Marginalised Mothers

Marginalised Mothers provides a detailed and much-needed insight into the lived experience of mothers who are frequently the focus of public concern and intervention, yet all too often have their voices and experiences overlooked. The book explores how they make sense of their lives with their children and families, position themselves within a context of inequality and vulnerability, and resist, subvert and survive material and social marginalisation.

This controversial text uses qualitative data from a selection of working-class mothers to highlight the opportunities and choices they face and to expose the middle-class assumptions that ground much contemporary family policy. It will be of interest to students and researchers in sociology, social work and social policy, as well as social workers and policymakers.

Val Gillies is a Senior Research Fellow in the Families and Social Capital Group at London South Bank University, UK.

Relationships & Resources
Series Editors: Janet Holland and Rosalind Edwards
London South Bank University

A key contemporary political and intellectual issue is the link between the relationships that people have and the resources to which they have access. When people share a sense of identity, hold similar values, trust each other and reciprocally do things for each other, this has an impact on the social, political and economic cohesion of the society in which they live. So, are changes in contemporary society leading to deterioration in the link between relationships and resources, or new and innovative forms of linking, or merely the reproduction of enduring inequalities? Consideration of relationships and resources raises key theoretical and empirical issues around change and continuity over time as well as time use, the consequences of globalisation and individualisation for intimate and broader social relations, and location and space in terms of communities and neighbourhoods. The books in this series are concerned with elaborating these issues and will form a body of work that will contribute to academic and political debate.

Other titles include:

Moving On
Bren Neale and Jennifer Flowerdew

Sibling Identity and Relationships: Sisters and Brothers
Rosalind Edwards, Lucy Hadfield, Helen Laucey and Melanie Mauthner

Teenagers and Citizenship: Experiences and Education
Susie Weller

Marginalised Mothers

Exploring working-class experiences of parenting

Val Gillies

 Routledge
Taylor & Francis Group

LONDON AND NEW YORK

First published 2007
by Routledge
2 Park Square, Milton Park, Abingdon, Oxon OX14 4RN

Simultaneously published in the USA and Canada
by Routledge
270 Madison Ave, New York, NY 10016

Routledge is an imprint of the Taylor & Francis Group, an informa business

Typeset in Sabon by
Keystroke, 28 High Street, Tettenhall, Wolverhampton
Printed and bound in Great Britain by
TJ International Ltd, Padstow, Cornwall

British Library Cataloguing in Publication Data
A catalogue record for this book is available from the British Library

Library of Congress Cataloging in Publication Data
Gillies, Val.
Marginalised mothers : exploring working class experiences of
parenting / Val Gillies.
p. cm. – (Relationships and resources series)
Includes bibliographical references and index.
1. Poor mothers–Great Britain–Social conditions. 2. Working class
women–Great Britain–Social conditions. 3. Marginalization,
Social–Great Britain. 4. Great Britain–Social conditions. I. Title.
HQ759.G498 2006
306.874'3086240941–dc22
2006020749

ISBN 10: 0–415–37635–1 (hbk)
ISBN 10: 0–415–37636–X (pbk)
ISBN 10: 0–203–96679–1 (ebk)

ISBN 13: 978–0–415–37635–8 (hbk)
ISBN 13: 978–0–415–37636–5 (pbk)
ISBN 13: 978–0–203–96679–2 (ebk)

Contents

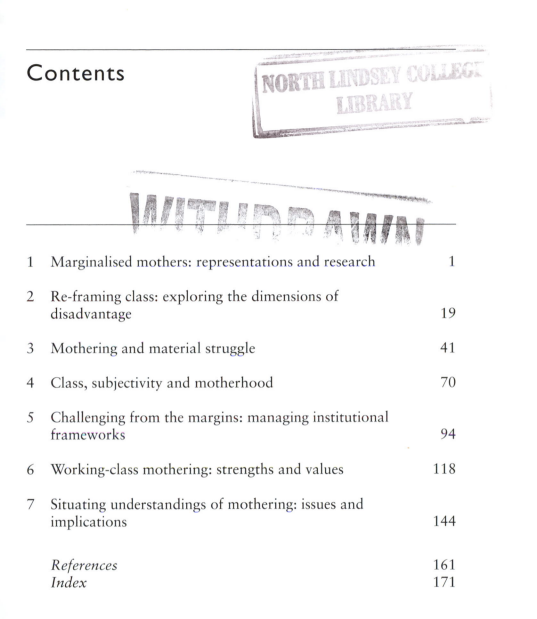

Chapter 1

Marginalised mothers

Representations and research

The consequences of poor parenting are all around in a constituency like mine: parents who don't value education as a route out of poverty, youngsters who learn and practise anti-social rather than social behaviour and, above all, the obvious and massive waste of unrealised human potential.

(Graham Allen, Labour Member of Parliament
for Nottingham North, *Guardian* 2004)

Nicky has five children by five different men . . . Nicky lives with her dishevelled-looking brood in an equally unkempt four-bedroom council house in Knowsley, Merseyside – known as Single Mother Central. Two-thirds of Knowsley is designated Green Belt, and not far away from the urban sprawl is glorious countryside dotted with wild flowers. Yet the number of single mothers grows ever higher. So what has gone wrong? Quite simply, when it comes to having children, Knowlsley exists in a moral vacuum. Tragically, it doesn't even occur to women such as Nicky Schiller that what they are doing might be wrong.

(Natalie Clarke, *Daily Mail* 2001)

Over the last few decades, attention and concern has focused on a particular sort of mother. She is portrayed as irresponsible, immature, immoral, and a potential threat to the security and stability of society as a whole. While this type of mother is accused of bad parenting, it is her status as poor and marginalised that sees her located at the centre of society's ills. From New Right to New Labour, tabloids to the broadsheets and daytime television to documentaries, working-class mothers who do not conform to standards grounded in middle-class privilege are vilified and blamed. While mothers have always been held responsible for behaviour and development, recent years have seen a cultural shift in the way parenting is conceptualised and targeted by policy-makers. Family relationships have traditionally been viewed as personal, private and immune from state intervention. This boundary is now regularly transgressed in an explicit and determined effort to mould and regulate individual subjectivity and citizenship at the level of the family. Parenting is no longer accepted as an interpersonal bond characterised by love and care. Instead it has been re-framed as a job requiring particular skills and expertise which must be taught by formally qualified professionals. Working class mothering practices are held up as the antithesis of good parenting, largely through their association with poor outcomes for children.

This book takes a more situated look at family lives that are so often misrepresented, disrespected and scapegoated. It will examine the particular challenges of poverty and low social status and will highlight the values and strengths that are generated in response. Based on qualitative interview research, the book will explore how working-class mothers make sense of their lives with their children, how they position themselves within a context of inequality and vulnerability, and how they resist, subvert and survive material and social marginalisation. I begin this chapter with a critical discussion of wider academic and policy debates around parenting to highlight the way that childrearing practices have come to be held accountable for crime, deprivation and inequality. More specifically I will show how mothering, as an activity and an identity, is understood and evaluated in relation to shifting, politicised notions of childhood and 'children's needs' (Lawler 2000; Phoenix and Woollett 1991). Drawing on research literature and policy documents, I argue that parenting prescriptions have become increasingly detached from the lives and experiences of those they are directed at. I will then describe the detailed qualitative studies that inform this book, outlining the approach and methods used and introducing the mothers whose stories feature throughout.

Parenting and the production of the subject

Family life has long been a political feeding ground. Fear of the social consequences of an emerging urban mass in the nineteenth century established a durable link between the wellbeing and rearing of children and the welfare of society as a whole. The perceived threat to the interests of the wealthy posed by those defined as 'degenerate', 'feeble minded' and 'morally corrupt' was associated with notions of nature and nurture, made popular by the early psychologist Francis Galton (Burman 1994). Products of poverty, such as crime, violence, vice and pauperism were medicalised and treated as defects of character to be controlled through a prophylactic inculcation of moral values (Rose 1989). The establishment of compulsory elementary schooling in the late 1800s reflected this concern to regulate children (Hendrick 1990). However, through the years the target of public intervention has largely shifted from children to mothers as guardians of their children's normal development (Lawler 2000; Walkerdine and Lucey 1989; Burman 1994). The discipline of developmental psychology emerged as a language to voice concerns about childrearing, warranting a range of ideological values on the grounds of scientific objectivity (Rose 1989). Mothers are positioned in relation to these values, with notions of acceptable parenting resting on constructions of childhood and children's needs that are conveyed through a developmental discourse.

As Erica Burman (1994) has argued, developmental psychology can be seen as an essentially political device, used to regulate both children and their parents. The notion of the 'normal' child exists as a production rather than a description, in that it is based on comparisons of scores and observations across age-graded populations. Although conceptions of normality are not based on real, existing children, they constitute the foundation for determining acceptable development and as such define notions of adequate parenting. For example, studies comparing children raised in non-traditional families to other children often begin by discussing the rise in family breakdown, emphasising how common it now is for children to be parented outside of a conventional nuclear family. Yet despite the increased incidence of non-traditional families, these children are still evaluated against a fixed notion of normality. Consequently, 'normal development', as constructed in developmental psychology texts, is a contradictory concept. While equated with naturalness or ordinary behaviour/ability, it is presented as a particularly fragile developmental achievement dependent on appropriate parenting. Nikolas Rose describes how the emergence of the child guidance clinic brought with it a new psychology which located social adjustment at a psychic level. He states:

> If families produced normal children, this was itself an accomplishment, not a given; it was because they regulated their emotional economy correctly. The production of normality now appeared to be a process fraught with pitfalls. The line between safety and danger was a narrow one; it was all too easy for major problems to develop from minor upsets if they were not handled correctly. A constant scrutiny of the emotional interchanges of family life was required, in the name of the mental hygiene of the individual and society.
>
> (Rose 1989: 155)

This regulation comprises far more than state intervention in the lives of poor or non-nuclear families. Childrearing practices which uphold the interests of the state have been increasingly and effectively operating through the subjective desires of parents wishing to optimise their children's development. Many writers have sought to demonstrate how power operates through, rather than in resistance to subjectivity, in that individuals are shaped and managed by their own feelings and emotional investments (Rose 1989, 2002; Foucault 1979; Donzelot 1979). Although direct and threatened coercion exists as a bottom line, a majority of families are often forced to produce and regulate themselves through dominant, ideologically charged discourses.

As Steph Lawler (2000) points out, mothering, as an activity and an identity, is understood and evaluated in relation to specific notions of child-hood and 'children's needs. This is despite evidence of the socially constructed nature of childhood as a concept (James *et al.* 1998; Woodhead 1997; Jenks 1996). As the work by the French historian Phillip Aries (1962) established, children beyond initial infant dependency were regarded as small adults until the separate status of childhood was developed between the fifteenth and eighteenth centuries. The concept of 'natural' childhood has been con-structed over several centuries as both an idea and a target, resulting in increasing state regulation and control of the young and their parents (Rose 1989, 2002). Over the years Western nations have evolved a set of highly complex measures to enforce conformity of development and thereby safeguard and reproduce existing power relations.

The contemporary politics of parenting

Good parenting in the home is more important than anything else to a child's future.

(Margerate Hodge, Minister for Children, 2004)

I can't raise people's children for them, and I can't personally go out on the street and make sure that everything is fine within the local community. What I can do, however, is give the police and the local authorities and those that need them the powers they need.

(Tony Blair, speech at the Meridian Community Centre in Watford 2005)

Heads call for 'beacon' parents
Tips on good parenting should be printed on the back of cereal packets and milk cartons, posted up on buses and shown on television, head teachers recommend. And the government should introduce 'beacon' parents, the naming and shaming of bad parents, parent achievement awards, a system of fines for parents who failed to meet their targets and child benefit bonuses for those who performed well. Heads say this may go some way to reducing the growing body of parents who consider it acceptable to abuse school staff.

(BBC News Online 2001)

The long history of state involvement in family life has reached new heights in recent decades. In the UK, parenting has been pushed to the centre stage of the policy curriculum in line with a neo-liberal emphasis on family, community and personal responsibility. Concerns about changes in the structure and status of family relationships in the 1960s and 1970s were viewed by many as an indication of a wider moral malaise needing urgent reform. However, it was during this time that more specific links were made between parenting and social *dis-ease* through the 'cycle of deprivation' theory. In the early 1970s, Secretary for State for Education in the UK conservative government, Keith Joseph, was a keen advocate of the theory, which suggested that poverty ran in families as a result of children inheriting values and lifestyles which lock them into permanent disadvantage (Joseph 1975). From the perspective of Joseph and other right-wing commentators, breaking this cycle of deprivation required a change in the attitudes and moral mindsets of poor parents. Although Joseph commissioned extensive research to prove that poverty was transmitted through families, he found the results to be disappointing. The theory lost credibility when his own study highlighted the significance of multiple structural factors as opposed to culture or attitude (Morris 1994).

Regardless of the evidence, the focus on the conduct of the deprived and disenfranchised was further developed in the 1980s by an emerging 'New Right' which sought to shift policy away from state assistance and towards moral regulation (Davies 1993; Dennis and Erdos 1992). In an echo of the Victorian concept of the 'undeserving poor', theorists such as Charles Murray proposed the existence of an 'underclass' populated by the feckless and workshy, and perpetuated through a 'culture of dependency' (Murray 1994). At the heart of the New Right critique was the challenge to patriarchal values embodied by changing family structures, which were seen as undermining the foundations of society. Women were portrayed as increasingly placing their own needs above those of their children and husbands, facilitated by the availability of welfare support enabling them to live independently. Women's liberation and welfare benefits were also seen as undermining men's incentive to work and provide for their families, encouraging them to abandon their domestic responsibilities.

From the perspective of the New Right, this lack of moral responsibility is inextricably linked to an economic decline associated with greater dependency on the welfare state and an unstable social order. Murray and many other proponents claimed that halting the growth of this emerging underclass was essential to prevent economic decline and suggested this could only be achieved through government policy which supports and enforces traditional family responsibility (Mead 1986; Murray 1994; Dennis and Erdos 1992; Davies 1993; Murray 1994). However, the family policy pursued by the UK Conservative government in the 1980s was contradictory and ambivalent, despite a preponderance of traditionalist, authoritarian rhetoric (Fox Harding 2000).

The Conservatives introduced the 'no fault' clause in divorce while they simultaneously demonised lone mothers as a threat to society. Policy measures focused largely on tightening social security entitlements and attempting to make absent fathers pay child support. The more intimate features of family life was seen as a distinct private sphere lying beyond the boundaries of legitimate state intervention by many conservatives. As J. Rodger (1995) has pointed out, the attempts to control and regulate behaviour of parents have always been at odds with the individualistic libertarian instincts of those positioned on the political right.

There was a renewed focus on the role of parents in the UK when the New Labour government in came to power in 1997. Drawing on a communitarian discourse as opposed to New Right rhetoric, the incoming government proclaimed its intention to prioritise families by placing them at the heart of the policy agenda (Wasoff and Hill 2002). While ostensibly distancing themselves from the more punitive aspects of conservative policy, New Labour developed a social democratic critique of individualism. The corroding influence of a 'me first' mentality was seen as undermining the co-operation and reciprocity necessary to sustain families and communities. Drawing on the work of Anthony Giddens (1991, 1998) and communitarian philosophers such as Amati Etzoni (1994), the New Labour government sought to address the perceived threat individualisation posed to family ties and social cohesion.

Their so called 'third way' approach aimed to balance individual rights with social responsibility through an emphasis on both moral tolerance and personal obligation. The wide-ranging and often conflicting policies that emerged were also heavily shaped by efforts to address general concerns about crime and public order (Gillies 2005a). Denoting a new focus on personal responsibility and the role of parenting in crime prevention, the prime minister to be, Tony Blair, campaigned for his leadership declaring 'the break-up of family and community bonds is intimately linked to the breakdown in law and order' (cited in Fairclough 2000: 42). This theme has been pursued over the years through regular moral panics about anti-social behaviour and the decline of 'respect', with poor parents depicted as uncaring, irresponsible and out of control.

An association between crime and upbringing is cited in a number of studies, implicating a variety of factors including ineffective discipline practices, lack of maternal support, low parental supervision and lack of attachment (Prior and Paris 2005; Farrington 1996; Graham and Bowling 1995). However, this research relies on simple linear models of causality, ignoring the complex range of factors that interact. As Cook (1997) notes, unemployment, low income and social deprivation remain the major risk factors precipitating an encounter with the criminal justice service. Attempts to determine other causal factors inevitably conflate the cause of crime with the features of those who have been defined as prime prone. Delinquency could easily be linked to any number of life variables, including gender, race, neighbourhood, unemployment etc., but a preoccupation with family relationships reflects a 'commonsense' view that deviancy is rooted in upbringing. As a result, policy-makers commission research to establish the family practices associated with crime but avoid seeking any detailed understanding of the behaviours in question (Gillies 2000).

While representations of poor parenting as a threat to society are long-standing, policy approaches in the UK have taken a new turn of late. More specifically, an emphasis on social justice is used to warrant intervention in the traditionally private sphere of the family on the basis that children who are parented well will have a better chance of upward social mobility. According to the British government, a range of factors are key in enabling children to break the 'cycle of deprivation' and overcome the effects of disadvantage (Home Office 2003b). These include strong relationships with parents, parental involvement with education, strong role models, feeling valued, and individual characteristics such as intelligence. Conspicuously absent from this list is any acknowledgement of material or financial capital as significant resources in evening-out life chances. In an apparent revival of the 'cycle of deprivation theory', the implication is that a quality upbringing is all that is needed to ensure equal opportunity (Gillies 2005b).

On the basis of this conviction, the government draws the conclusion that poor parents are failing to impart the necessary skills and traits that are needed to sustain a just society. They argue that in order to address inequality, childrearing must be repositioned as a public rather than a private concern, and the state must take responsibility for inculcating the practice of good parenting. It is reasoned that only the political right argues for childrearing to remain the private concern of families, while a more enlightened New Labour government recognises its moral duty to uphold social justice (Hodge 2004). For the sake of their children's future, and for the stability and security of society as a whole, working-class parents must be taught how to raise children who are capable of becoming middle class. The significance accorded to parenting as a crucial determinant of children's future life chances has been followed through with a range of policy initiatives designed to 'support' parents in their essential practice. For the most part this has been in the form of guidance and education, rather than practical or material help. The term 'parenting support' has become a common shorthand description for parenting classes, where mothers are sent to learn 'childrearing skills' (Gillies 2005a). As Frank Ferudi (2001) notes, this is part of a creeping professionalisation of family life based on the notion that parenting can be distilled into a series of detachable, universally applicable skills.

Caring for children is generally viewed as a classless activity (Duncan 2005), and as such parenting 'support' initiatives are presented as relevant resources for all families. The gender neutral term 'parent' also suggests the joint involvement of fathers as well as mothers. In practice, though, such initiatives are targeted at poor and disadvantaged mothers. For example, the British government's flagship parenting support programme 'Sure Start', based on the American 'Head Start' scheme, is concentrated in areas of high deprivation and is described as a cornerstone of the government's drive to tackle child poverty and social exclusion. Sure Start is a much praised community-based programme offering a range of services including health advice and parenting classes, with its publicly stated intention being:

> to promote the physical, intellectual and social development of babies and young children – particularly those who are disadvantaged – so that they can flourish at home and when they get to school, and thereby break the cycle of disadvantage for the current generation of young children.
> (http://www.surestart.gov.uk/aboutsurestart/)

From this perspective, disadvantage faced by poor families is a personal, developmental issue rather than a consequence of inequality (Gillies 2005b). With social and economic marginalisation explained at the level of the developing individual, working-class mothers can be blamed as too ignorant or plain lazy to pass on social betterment skills. The twin concerns of criminal and social justice are now regularly drawn on to present a powerful moral case for intervening and controlling the parenting practices of working-class families. Unregulated, poor parents spawn damaged, anti-social children destined to live a life of poverty and crime, while those made aware of their responsibilities are empowered to re-write their family's destiny. On the basis of this reasoning only the most selfish, uncaring or stupid would reject advice and guidance designed to improve their children's life chances. But as I will show in the following chapters, there are a range of complex and situation-specific reasons why working-class mothers are unable to engage with the values and practices that are promoted.

Nevertheless, the moral justification for parenting classes ensures that the 'support' offered to disadvantaged families is becoming increasingly coercive and authoritarian. This is characterised in UK family policy by a punitive approach towards parents described by the Home Office as 'unwilling or unable to respond to support when offered' (Home Office 2003b: 9). Sanctions include the fining of parents whose children commit crimes, miss school or misbehave in the classroom, and the imprisonment of parents of persistent truants. Government consultation papers contain even more severe proposals, including benefit cuts for errant families, the removal of persistent young offenders from their families for placement in foster homes, and the committal of parents to residential homes for 're-training' (Home Office 2003b). This social and political context frames the lives of the mothers featured in this book. It also informs and warrants the actions of social workers, health visitors, teachers and other professionals, while filtering into popular culture and the mass media. The result is a powerful web of discourses which position working-class mothers as inferior, irresponsible or even dangerous.

Parenting or mothering?

Although raising children is still a predominantly female responsibility, the gender neutral term 'parenting' has now largely replaced references to mothering. This reflects a cultural shift in ideas about childrearing and a more general understanding that men have the same potential as women to care for children. Over time images of fatherhood have also altered from traditional conceptions of distant authority figures to involved, active carers. Fathers are now constructed in policy and legal terms as fulfilling a crucial role in meeting children's emotional needs. Carefully worded references to 'parenting' in social policy documents seek to acknowledge men's role in childrearing as significant, and are underpinned by concerns about the consequences of absent or distant fathers (Williams 1998). More specifically, involved fathers are identified as a key factor in protecting against juvenile criminal behaviour (Home Office 1998).

Yet discussions of 'parenting' can obscure the fact that caring for children remains a highly gendered practice. Mothers tend to maintain primary responsibility for the day-to-day care of their children, while fathering is something the majority of men are forced to fit around full time work (Ribbens McCarthy et al. 2003). As Steph Lawler (2000) notes, it might be argued that anyone can mother, but understandings of what makes a good mother are distinctly feminised. Parenting classes are in the main designed and targeted at mothers (Moran et al. 2004) and focus on characteristics most associated with women, such as sensitivity, communication and warmth. Significantly, it is also mothers who bear the brunt of sanctions designed to enforce 'good parenting'. As research conducted by Mark Drakeford (1996) reveals, court orders attempting to make parents accountable for their children's misdemeanours are invariably served on mothers, even on the occasions when the fathers are also present.

With little real change in the status and responsibilities accorded to mothers and fathers (Bruegel and Gray 2004), inclusive references to parenting objectify the nature of childrearing as caring labour and obscure its acutely gendered status. Recent efforts at the level of policy to encourage men to become more involved in parenting risks further marginalising working-class mothers. As Jonathan Scourfield and Mark Drakeford (2002) argue, family policies ushered in by the New Labour government are based on optimism about men in the home and pessimism about women in the home. For example, legislation entitling fathers to unpaid leave is underpinned by the assumption that fathers will forgo their salaries to spend time with their children. More disturbingly, there is little recognition that family life is constituted through gendered and generational power dynamics. The serious threat that some fathers might pose to women and children is barely recognised (Featherstone and Trinder 2001). Despite the unequal burden of responsibility shouldered by mothers, fathers' rights groups have garnered public and political sympathy with their portrayal of family courts as inherently biased towards mothers. Contemporary legal frameworks, however, clearly construct fathers as central to children's needs (Children and Adoption Bill 2005). Meanwhile, in the UK mothers are viewed as posing a problem if they remain at home in a full-time caring capacity at the taxpayer's expense (Scourfield and Drakeford 2002). Efforts to 'support' or coerce lone mothers on benefits into employment highlight a major tension in a policy approach which purports to prioritise parenting responsibility (Featherstone and Trinder 2001).

While this book is in no way belittling or downplaying the significance of working-class fathers, its focus on mothering reflects the very different experiences and expectations associated with each role. While the effects of gender pervade every aspect of our lives, motherhood brings the inequality between men and women most sharply into view. Notions of what it means to be a mother are still bound up with culturally ingrained assumptions about nature, biology and responsibility, and consequently all women are to some extent defined by their relation to motherhood. Even childless women are positioned by these discourses, viewed as either potential mothers, failed childbearers or as just plain selfish (Phoenix and Woollett 1991). As Valerie Walkerdine and Helen Lucey (1989) note, public discourses of motherhood tell us a great deal about our social landscape and its prevailing efforts to guarantee liberal democracy through the labour of women. They point out that by examining routine details of domestic and childrearing practices we reveal 'fundamental questions about the production of democracy, about freedom and about women's oppression' (Walkerdine and Lucey 1989: 33). These questions become ever more crucial when the particular injustices facing working-class mothers are foregrounded.

The research framework

Two research studies are drawn on to inform this book. The first was conducted as part of my PhD thesis, which was based on an in-depth exploration of working-class mothers parenting outside of conventional nuclear family boundaries. The second study focused on parenting resources and was carried out with Professor Rosalind Edwards several years later as part of the Economic and Research Council (ESRC)-funded Families & Social Capital project. I will describe each project in more detail before I outline how they form the basis for the following chapters.

Marginalised mothers: social subjectivities and material positionings

Based on single intensive interviews with five white, working-class mothers who do not live with the fathers of their children, this study was written up as my PhD thesis in 2002. The aim was to convey the complex, situation-specific nature of personal understandings and actions by focusing, in turn, on the five mothers' accounts of their lives. The women who took part in the study were accessed through my own personal contacts. While all five were parenting outside of conventional nuclear family boundaries, their individual experiences differed considerably in terms their personal histories, the number of children they have, the status of their relationships and the practical resources that are available to them.

The mothers were all white, lived in areas with high deprivation indexes, and had limited access to financial resources. The uniform ethnicity of this small sample was not a deliberate research decision, but instead reflects the make-up of my personal networks and the difficulty I encountered in reaching working-class ethnic minority families. My position as a white researcher with a working-class background and social networks meant that I found it relatively easy to access white, working-class mothers willing to be interviewed, but this was not the case with black and ethnic minority mothers. With no one to introduce me or vouch for my motives, my approaches were met with suspicion and polite refusal. As has been the experience of other white researchers, I was interpreted as a white, institutional figure (Edwards 1996; Gillies 2004).

The mothers' own particular accounts are analysed in detail, chapter by chapter, in the thesis, revealing the different discourses and frameworks of meaning each drew upon to conceptualise her life with her children. While it is not possible in this book to reproduce the mothers' stories in the same depth, their lives and experiences feature substantially. As such I will briefly introduce each mother before moving on to outline the second study informing this book. As with all the accounts discussed in this book, names and other identifying factors have been changed:

Sarah lives on the outskirts of a major town in a housing association flat with her 7-year-old daughter, Lisa. Sarah had split up with Lisa's father, Tony, and had begun a new long-distance relationship with a Greek man she met while on holiday. Tony, a motor mechanic, has regular contact with his daughter. Sarah depends on state benefits and contributions from Tony.

Liz lives with her partner, Eddie, in a ex-council house in a suburb. Eddie, a painter and decorator, is the father of Liz's youngest son, 4-year-old Calum, who was born shortly after Liz and the boys first moved in with Eddie. Liz had been previously married to Pete, during which time she had two sons, Scott aged 10 and Adam aged 13. Pete still sees his sons every weekend.

Sam   lives on welfare benefits in a council house in with her 2½-year-old son Joe and her 6-year-old daughter Sophie. Sam had left the children's father, Kevin, several years ago after he developed a drug dependency and became violent. Kevin has sporadic but regular contact with the children.

Nina   lives in council flat with her 10-year-old daughter, Amy. Nina split up with Amy's father, Bill, after he became violent and began disappearing for months at a time. Amy has had virtually no contact with him since. Nina works in a disabled day centre while Amy attends school.

Sally   lives in a four-bedroom council house with her partner, Ian, and five of her seven children, the eldest two having left home. Ricky (20), Mel (18) and Andy (16), share Sally's first husband as their father, while the other four children, Joel (12), Jamie (11), Brad (10), and Jack (9) are from Sally's second marriage. Each weekend Ian's 6-year-old daughter Kelly also comes to stay. Ian works nights as a caretaker, while Sally is employed full time in a children's nursery.

Resources in parenting: access to capitals

The second study informing this book was concerned with the micro-processes of family life and focused more generally on parenting resources. This research had two phases, with the first based on an extensive National Opinion Poll (NOP) omnibus survey of parents of children aged 8 to 12, and the second involving follow-up intensive interviews with 25 mothers and 11 fathers from a wide range of 27 households across England and Scotland (see Edwards and Gillies 2005 for further details of the research design). The first *survey* phase of this research was carried out to determine consensus, or lack of it, in parents' publicly expressed norms about appropriate sources of support. The second *intensive* phase of our research involved pursuing what resources parents themselves draw on and provide in the complex and specific circumstances that face them in their own lives. Data from this latter qualitative phase is drawn on throughout this book to illustrate the particular experiences of working-class mothers.

Definitions and theories of social class will be discussed at length in Chapter 2, but in short these mothers had low incomes, lacked formal educational qualifications, and lived and socialised in disadvantaged communities. The method of accessing families for the *Resources in Parenting* study through an extensive, door-to-door omnibus survey generated a relatively large pool of parents willing to take part in the qualitative phase of the research. Consequently we were able to locate and include ethnic minority parents who volunteered to participate. This explains the more ethnically diverse make-up of this additional sample of nine mothers and enables a more considered exploration of the way class gender and ethnicity are entwined. Again, I will briefly introduce these mothers to contextualise the use of their experiences throughout the book:

Denise is white and lives with her husband Ted and their 10-year-old son Liam in a rented house on the outskirts of a densely populated urban area. Ted works long shifts Monday to Saturday as a cleaner in a local shopping centre, while Denise cares for Liam and provides unpaid childcare for a friend's 18-month-old girl.

Julie is an African-Caribbean lone mother of two children by different fathers. Her youngest daughter, Carly, is 10 and her older son, Lloyd, is 15. She also provides regular unpaid childcare for her sister's children. She rents a housing association flat on a purpose-built estate in a densely populated urban area and draws state benefits. The children have very limited contact with their fathers.

Kelly is a white mother of a 9-year-old son, Craig, and a 7-year-old daughter, Jenna. The children's father was violent and abusive and they were forced to flee to a women's refuge to escape him. They now live with Kelly's new partner, Terry, and his 6-year-old daughter Jess, in a rented house in a small town. Terry works as a lorry driver while Kelly cares full time for the children.

Meena is an Indian mother of three sons. She came to England in the early 1990s with her husband Sal and her first son Rega, who is now 11. She went on to have Hanif (9) and Atta (2). Both Meena and Sal are employed as contract cleaners and work alternate shifts for the minimum wage. They live in a council flat on the outskirts of a densely populated city.

Paula is white and lives with her husband Barry and their two daughters Ellie (12) and Rosie (6), in a rural part of the country. They have bought the council house they live in. Having previously worked in factories, Paula and Barry have set up a mail order business from home which requires them to work long hours.

Annette is an African-Caribbean lone mother with two daughters, Melissa (16) and Isis (12). She rents a housing association property in an inner-city area. She works full time as a receptionist, Monday to Friday, and has applied for a Saturday job because she is struggling to pay off debts. The children have no contact with their biological father, but see Annette's previous partner regularly.

Louise is white and lives with her partner Gary and their two children, Lucy (8) and Josh (6). Louise works part time as an admin. assistant and Gary works full time as a bus driver. When Gary's wages improved they gave up their council flat to buy a house in a semi-rural town.

Carol is white and lives with her partner Simon and her two children in a council house in a rural area. Simon is the father of 4-year-old Shannon, while 10-year-old Todd is from Carol's previous relationship and no longer sees his father. Simon works for a large engineering company, but is facing the threat of redundancy. Carol cares for the children and works part time as a cleaner.

Naomi is a Sudanese refugee and lives with her husband Daniel and two daughters, Rebecca (10) and Ruth (9). The family are devout Christians and were forced to fee their country of origin after government persecution. For three years they have been living in a house in an inner city. This is temporary accommodation provided by the council and they are aware that they may be asked to move at short notice. The family are dependent on welfare benefits as Daniel suffers from poor health and is unable to work.

These nine mothers were drawn from a wider research sample of considerably better-off parents. While the more advantaged families in the *Resources in Parenting* project are not discussed in any depth in this book, I will at various times draw on their very different experiences to provide a useful and telling contrast. These comparisons highlight the extent to which personal and cultural values underpinning parenting are grounded in social and economic conditions. They also demonstrate how normative, family policy measures are rooted in middle-class privilege with little appreciation of life as it is lived by working-class mothers and their children.

Relations of research: eliciting accounts and representing lives

As Valerie Hey notes, 'research is always at some level about seeking and in part claiming an understanding of the other' (Hey 2000: 161). This study represents my attempt, as a researcher, to hear, interpret and produce an analytical account of these women's lives. Although my conception of the relationship between the researcher and the researched eschews traditional subject/object divides, I am not warranting my analysis on the grounds of empathy or interpersonal affinity. Any attempt to give research participants a 'voice', either by translating their views or by speaking out on their behalf, reflects the researcher's interpretation, which is inevitably grounded in their own subjective and material reality. The 'knowledge' I have produced in this book derives, in part, from my own culture, history, location and investment as a researcher. These factors influenced who I interviewed (and who I was able to interview), what questions I asked and what interpretations I have made. Each interview generated a particular story of being a mother and caring for children. Questions and prompts were specific to each interview, generating unique accounts. The following chapters do not seek to reproduce the women's words or to represent them in any essential way. The chapters of this book were produced through a process of intensive interpretation and analysis, and while this inevitably required the application of my own framework of meaning, the data that emerged profoundly challenged many of my personal assumptions and perspectives.

Christine Griffin points out that when we speak for others we cannot become them, we can only tell our story about their lives (Griffin 1996). This recognition of the researcher's role in constructing 'knowledge' has provoked numerous debates about the politics of 'representing the other'. According to Kitzinger and Wilkinson, 'claims to objectivity and universality of representation have been shown to be the alibis of the powerful – the powerful among women as much as the powerful among men' (1996: 10). Feminist researchers often emphasise the commonalities between themselves and the participants of their research as a validation of their right to represent other women. Nevertheless, structural and individual differences inevitably outweigh similarities. As such there can be no 'authentic' basis for representative research, even when specific experiences or identities are shared by researcher and researched. As Diane Reay notes, 'Identification can result in a denial of the power feminist researchers exercise in the selection and interpretation of data' (1996: 57).

Conducting the interviews* and analysing the resulting transcripts were processes marked by implicit and explicit recognitions and dis-identifications between myself and the mothers. My working-class background and its embodied residues (such as my London accent and style of speech) combined with my personal contacts in some of the mother's social networks generated an important basis for negotiating access. These 'credentials' meant that in some cases I was likely to be regarded as a connected outsider rather than a middle-class, institutional figure. Nevertheless, the contrast between my life and the lives of the mothers I interviewed was visible and undeniable. But while it is vital to recognise issues of power and difference, it is also important to acknowledge identification and connection as fundamental to inter-subjective and intra-subjective meaning. As Valerie Hey points out:

> Power cannot be appeased primarily if at all by practices of abstract intellectualisation. What is required is a different sort of risk taking – one of taking up (invariably normative) positions through seeking empirical investigations of real people in recognisable situations. The rush to distance from the 'other' is I think closing down of the responsibility for knowing and knowledge production of the self and 'other'. The really difficult challenge is to work the space between us/them/you/me/self/other and to articulate points of connection and disconnection as these are secured in relations of power, in order to argue for their change. Not to do so merely secures the prevailing hierarchies.
>
> (Hey 2000: 179)

While this book contains my telling of the mother's stories, it also represents an approach to research that perceives the 'other' as always connected with the 'same' (Hey 2000). Rather than basing my claims to 'knowledge' on authentic research encounters, I am generating explicitly political under-standings of the mother's experiences by exploring the networks of power which position all individuals (including researchers) and constitute human relations.

Structure of the book

Following on from this introduction to the issues, Chapter 2 will set out the theoretical context of the book. More specifically, the concept of class will be outlined in order to highlight its central place in shaping the experience of mothering. Theories of class will be critically reviewed in the context of the contemporary emphasis on individualisation, detraditionalisation and

---

* I conducted most but not all of the interviews. In the *Resources in Parenting* sample, Anna Einasdottir interviewed Denise and Julie.

social exclusion. It will be argued that while poverty and inequality remain as pervasive as ever, there has been a reconfiguration of class representations in terms of personal and moral distinctions. The chapter will outline an alternative understanding of class as a social construct with very real material effects, and will show how being a working-class mother means being positioned by categorisations and representations that actively uphold and maintain structural inequalities. The chapter will also highlight the way that class, gender and ethnicity fuse in the pathologisation and delegitimisation of working-class mothering practices.

Chapter 3 moves on to consider working-class mothers' personal stories of coping with disadvantage. It will show how obtaining sufficient money and securing decent housing were consuming imperatives, shaping biographies and experiences of motherhood. By focusing on specific examples, the chapter will explore the consequences for parenting of a struggle to survive with very little money, power or security. A range of experiences will be explored alongside a more detailed consideration of three stories to illustrate the particular challenges faced by individual mothers. In this chapter I demonstrate how social, physical and material factors frame decisions and actions, severely limiting choice and aspiration.

Chapter 4 explores the relationship between class, selfhood and personal values. Notions of 'good parenting' are strongly tied to particular understandings of development and subjectivity. This chapter will explore the disjuncture between normative models of the self and working-class experiences. By drawing on specific examples from mothers' accounts, it will challenge middle-class individualist values, showing how mothering on the margins is characterised by a pressure to raise children who fit in rather than stand out. It will also argue that working-class families are used as markers of individual failure, enabling the middle classes to distinguish themselves as rational, autonomous, reflexive selves and thereby claim a natural entitlement to privilege.

In Chapter 5 institutional frameworks of regulation are examined through an exploration of working-class mothers' experiences of dealing with middle-class professionals. This chapter examines the way middle-class values are institutionalised and enforced through professional discourses, and draws on particular examples to highlight the social and cultural disparities inherent in encounters between professionals and marginalised mothers. The chapter will analyse specific mothers' accounts of their children's poor academic performance, disruptive behaviour in the classroom, truancy and juvenile delinquency to reveal how situated meanings clash with institutional expectations.

Attention shifts in Chapter 6 to a consideration of the crucial cultural and emotional resources that working-class mothers provide in enabling their children to survive in a context of material deprivation. It will examine how demands and pressures are met by working-class mothers in the every-day course of caring for their children and will draw out the situated nature of decisions and practices. The chapter will also demonstrate how motherhood generates a positive identity for working-class women, symbolising knowledge, self-worth, strength, power and resilience. In particular, public concerns around young and lone mothers will be contrasted with real lived experience to demonstrate how pride, satisfaction and pleasure interrupt and subvert social stigma.

The concluding chapter reviews the issues that have been raised in the book as a whole, and argues for a greater understanding of and respect for working-class mothers. It draws together and develops the theme of situated mothering practices and emphasises the vital importance of material and economic resources in shaping actions, decisions and experiences. In particular, it argues that public and policy debates around parenting should pay closer attention to the grounded nature of meaning and experience. In calling for a new approach that recognises the strength, commitment and value of working-class mothering, this chapter makes the case for abandoning efforts to inculcate 'parenting skills'. Instead it emphasises the significance of financial, practical and material support in addressing the root causes of marginalisation.

Chapter 2

Re-framing class

Exploring the dimensions of disadvantage

For the last few decades class has been the elephant in the room. It clearly exists as a potent and prevailing social distinction, but is rarely explicitly articulated or acknowledged as such. As Andrew Sayer (2005) notes, it is an embarrassing and unsettling subject which often might be considered rude or insensitive to mention. Many prefer to see class as an old-fashioned concept associated with a bygone age. Decline in the UK manufacturing base has destabilised traditional working-class communities, with industrial capitalism giving way to a new globalised economy in which a general rhetoric of 'classlessness' flourishes. Yet at the same time there has been a sharp polarisation of wealth in Britain, with research documenting how the rich and poor continue to live in very different worlds (Wheeler *et al.* 2005). In this chapter I draw on an emerging body of theoretical work to argue that class as a social indicator is more important than ever.

I begin by examining sociological conceptions of class and their critiques. I show how ideas have shifted away from dominant fixations on structure and stratification towards a more complex engagement with culture, subjectivity and power. This new focus on how class is lived explores changes in the way inequality is understood and experienced, while reasserting its crucial significance. In contrast to early, male-centred, sociological pre-occupations with employment and economic relationships, I show how this approach is well suited to exploring the lives of women who are mothers. As Simon Duncan points out, mothering is commonly assumed to be a classless practice (1995). In this chapter I demonstrate how motherhood is central to contemporary individualised and codified representations of class, with disadvantaged mothers depicted as ignorant, promiscuous, uncaring, irresponsible and most significantly, undeserving. Without the language of class to explain their lives, such mothers are set apart, misinterpreted and ultimately blamed for the social and economic marginalisation that characterises their lives. I show how a drawing back from class as an explanatory framework has seen the re-casting of disadvantage as moral disease passed on through the family.

Having made a case for the fundamental importance of class, the chapter moves on to address more practical questions about how we might identify and make sense of classed practices. Central to this process is the recognition that class as a lived experience is necessarily fused with other categories and identities. Inequality is the product of a range of social factors, with gender, race and ethnicity similarly powerful in exerting influence over access to resources. The way these crucial social divisions cross-cut and intersect will be considered, before setting out the pragmatic model of class I am using in my analysis of the accounts given by the mothers taking part in the research.

The fall and rise of class theory

Class has traditionally been a central analytic tool drawn on by social scientists to made sense of the workings and structure of society. In Britain, the study of class, or more particularly working-class communities, was a major focus through which sociology was established as a discipline in the 1960s (Savage 2000). Early work was primarily quantitative and orientated towards studying employment relations with emphasis placed on objectively measuring and categorising. As soon became clear, this approach to class was beset with difficulties and inconsistencies. Feminists pointed to the inability of a work-centred theory to conceptualise properly the place of women, while debates raged about classification criteria. There is no general agreement over what constitutes a definitive measurement of social class, and consequently various classification scales exist, placing emphasis on different indicators. For example, one of the most popular methods, the Registrar General's classification, defines individuals on the basis of their occupation. Socio-economic indexes take income to be a main indicator of class, while other scales use a combination of occupation, economic status, education and housing status (Osborne and Morris 1979).

Critiques of class theory were compounded by a rival sociological preoccupation with social change which emphasised a dramatically altered social and economic landscape. New theories emerged describing how industrial capitalism has been replaced a 'post-industrial' society in which old notions of class are no longer relevant (Gorz 1982). This transformation is viewed as having precipitated a new age of modernity, replacing the old predictabilities and certainties of industrial society, and bringing with it new risks and opportunities (Beck 1992; Beck and Beck-Gernsheim 1995, 2002). Such theories describe a de-traditionalisation and individualisation of social life, claiming a new significance for personal agency in negotiating and managing life events (Giddens 1991, 1992; Beck 1992; Beck and Beck-Gernsheim 2002). According to prominent sociological theorists like Anthony Giddens and Ulrick Beck, the demise of class and other group identities are characteristic of the new individualised lifestyles of late modern social actors (Giddens 1998; Beck 1992). While it is acknowledged that inequality remains, this is attributed to the individual rather than explained in terms of a particular group or class (Furlong and Cartmel 1997; Savage 2000).

By the late 1980s, class as an analytical category had largely fallen from favour. Theories emphasising choice and risk dominated the academic agenda, while the term 'social exclusion' all but replaced the term 'class' in the public and political lexicon. As Mike Savage (2000) points out, this was a period of unprecedented inequality, characterised by a virtual silence on the topic of class. Beverley Skeggs (1997) describes how this recoil from class occurred across a range of academic sites, with 'retreatists' either ignoring or denying its relevance. This was reinforced by an emphasis on other forms of social discrimination such as gender, race, sexuality and disability, often at the expense of class (Sayer 2005). Drawing on observations from bell hooks (2000), Andrew Sayer notes how:

> The liberal, affluent, educated whites regard treating others unequally on the basis of their gender, 'race' or sexuality as immoral, and they presumably realise that if they were to be sexist, racist or homophobic, they would themselves be responsible for reproducing injustice and undeserved inequality. They do not, however, see class inequality as unjust and probably do not regard it as their responsibility either.
>
> (Sayer 2005: 13)

The complex and discomforting nature of class encourages those who are privileged enough to ignore it (Skeggs 1997). Of late, though, there has been something of a renaissance in class theorising. This has been led in the main by feminist sociologists (many from working-class backgrounds) who have drawn out the real lived experience of class and reasserted its contemporary relevance. The work of the French sociologist Pierre Bourdieu (discussed in more detail further on in this chapter) has been fundamental in shaping this regeneration, providing a theoretical framework for new understandings of class distinction and reproduction (Devine and Savage 2005; Adkins and Skeggs 2005). These new approaches rely on a more nuanced perspective of social class as dynamic, symbolic and culturally produced. More specifically they highlight the way sociological theories of class are themselves actively implicated in cultural processes of classification and distinction.

For example, Beverley Skeggs (1997, 2004) notes how the historical generation of class as a categorisation has resulted in the production of distinctions which both warrant and project onto structural inequality. As she explains:

> Class is a discursive, historically specific construction, a product of middle-class political consolidation, which includes elements of fantasy and projection. The historical generation of classed categorizations provide discursive frameworks which enable, legitimate and map onto

material inequalities. Class conceptualizations are tautological in that positioning by categorizations and representation influence access to economic and cultural resources.

(Skeggs 1997: 5)

According to Lynette Finch (1993), the category of 'working class' derived from the attempts of those holding power and privilege to fortify and maintain their position. The middle classes came to distinguish and distance themselves from the working-class 'masses' who they regarded as having a dangerous potential for social disorder. This differentiation was further consolidated by technologies and practices which enabled surveillance, and thereby control of the working-class subject. The development of instruments enabling the measurement and categorisation of the working classes in the form of demographic statistics, social surveys, school and medical records, marked the beginning of the 'classing gaze' (Finch 1993). Working-class women, and more specifically working-class mothers, have consistently been at the forefront of this gaze ever since.

The emergence of class as a tool of social control has a number of consequences for those pathologised by it. In her longitudinal ethnographic study of a group of working-class women, Beverly Skeggs (1997) shows how lives are shaped by efforts not to appear working class. For these women the term 'working class' represented all that was worthless, polluted and vulgar, and consequently class, as a signifier, was central to the construction of subjectivities. Class was experienced as an exclusion by the women because they had no access to the financial and cultural resources to become part of the 'respectable' middle classes. Skeggs demonstrates how respectability is a key device by which women are classed through appearance, behaviour and childrearing. As a signifier it is implicitly linked to moral authority, with its lack translating into low social status and delegitimation. Gaining respectability is an important means of obtaining social worth and legitimacy, but without access to money and middle-class 'knowledge', working-class women are destined to live with the insecurity of their social position. As Skeggs states:

> Class becomes internalized as an intimate form of subjectivity, experienced as knowledge of always not being 'right'.

(Skeggs 1997: 90)

Skeggs does not suggest that the women in her study actively wanted to be like the middle class. On the contrary, she shows how their descriptions of encounters with the middle class were often characterised by criticism and ridicule. But efforts still were made by the women to avoid being positioned by a discourse that represents them as lazy, ugly, stupid and dangerous.

The individualisation of inequality

In moving away from viewing class as a distinct entity, theorists have detailed how social and cultural changes are characterised by new class formations. For example, Mike Savage (2000) has explored how the individualistic, de-traditionalised identities associated with contemporary societies remain highly classed. He shows how influential sociological accounts of the reflexive, late modern agent fail to engage with the principle that individualisation is dependant on a process of social distinction, linked to the ability to access resources. Legitimate (middle-class) selves and lives are still constructed from privilege and validated at the expense of others (Skeggs 2005). Yet through a denial of class, these individualisation theories have generated an ideologically powerful new language to explain personal experience and social relationships. Their influence has been particularly substantial in shaping the political landscape, underpinning an agenda of policy reform aimed at redistributing possibilities as opposed to wealth (Giddens 1998).

According to the prominent sociologist Anthony Giddens (1998), achieving a more equal and just society requires people to embrace their individualised citizenship and become 'responsible risk-takers'. From this perspective prosperity derives from becoming the right kind of self, while poverty and disadvantage is associated with poor self-management. Efforts to 'empower' individuals by ensuring that they take responsibility for their decisions has driven recent welfare policy in the UK, with emphasis placed on generating opportunities as opposed to direct financial or material aid (Dwyer 2002).

This highly individualised approach is evident in the language of 'social exclusion' now used to describe working-class disadvantage. As Ruth Levitas (1998) and Norman Fairclough (2000) argue, this approach marginalises notions of fairness and justice through the construction of a culturally distinct 'excluded' minority as the major, legitimate focus of concern for governments. Inequalities amongst the 'included' majority are then normalised, with both the privileges of the rich and the struggles of the poor rationalised through reference to an inclusive society. Rather than addressing the root problem of inequality, the moral choices of the privileged are normalised to warrant the regulation of the disadvantaged. Those unable or unwilling to conform to such dominant values are exceptionalised, positioned as outside the common fold; 'described but not explained' (Rose 1999: 488).

Constructed as a distinct condition suffered by individuals and communities, rather than a process characterised by a series of interlinked social problems, exclusion is portrayed as a problem in its own right, requiring 'more than' the re-distribution of wealth (Fairclough 2000). Consequently social exclusion is re-framed as a kind of disease affecting the least able and willing, with policy remedies orientated towards re-attaching the afflicted through modification of their lifestyle and conduct (Gillies 2005a). Thus, poverty and privilege, once discussed in terms of wealth distribution and attached to the concept of class, have been redefined by inclusion exclusion debates, which sideline issues of inequality and foreground, individual life-choices and conduct. Lack of material resources is then represented as a symptom of exclusion rather than its cause.

As such the concept of social exclusion shares many similarities with the New Right 'underclass' discourse, even though many commentators began using it in an attempt to counter moralism by emphasising the isolation experienced by those consistently denied opportunities (Levitas 1998). Public and political discourse slips backwards and forwards between the two poles of this debate, citing disadvantage and lack of opportunity as a target, while also accusing the marginalised of excluding themselves by refusing to accept personal responsibility. As was outlined in Chapter 1, such individualised understandings of disadvantage and inequality are reflected in the contemporary preoccupation with regulating parenting. Jock Young (1999) notes how the discourse of social exclusion invokes an imperative of inclusion. Exclusion is morally unacceptable, particularly where children are concerned. As a result, excluded parents (invariably mothers) must be supported or coerced back into the ranks of the included through paid employment and parenting classes. With no meaningful framework to understand the social and structural features of marginalised lives, there is an assumption that sheer force of will should be sufficient to override the effects of deprivation.

The displacement of class has been further compounded by a general shift towards an increasingly individualised identity politics in broader struggles for social justice (Skeggs 2004). As Nancy Fraser (1997) argues, class politics based on egalitarian redistribution of resources and goods have been overshadowed by a alternative (but not mutually exclusive) political goal aimed at promoting the recognition of difference, particularly in terms of gender, ethnicity and sexuality. This approach relies on an understanding of injustice as grounded in social interactions, interpretations and meanings. From this perspective, racism, sexism and homophobia are viewed in terms of a refusal of legitimacy and value, and are challenged through reclaiming and celebrating identities. Demands for recognition and resources are thus channelled through personal claims to oppressed identities. But as Andrew Sayer (2005) points out, the working class want to evade their poverty rather than have it affirmed, legitimised and celebrated. The redistribution they require necessitates more concrete action to relinquish privilege. As Sayer states:

> An egalitarian politics of recognition at the level of professed attitudes is easier for the well-off to swallow than an egalitarian politics of recognition-through-distribution, and it suits them to regard the former as progressive and the latter as passé, indeed the former can be a source of kudos. In fact, in seems that in British political culture over the last three decades, the more everyone is discursively acknowledged as being

of equal worth, the less the pressure to change the distribution of material goods, because the inequality of the latter is increasingly seen as a separate matter.

(Sayer 2005: 64)

The dominance of recognition politics effectively disenfranchises the working class from political struggle (Skeggs 2004). A prevailing silence on class as a social and structural phenomena leads to a personalisation of poverty and pejorative judgements against the poor, who are more likely to avoid public recognition of their identity. Unlike other social categories, class is bound up with shame and stigma and operates underneath the surface of social life producing and shaping lives.

Codifications of class

While rarely explicitly articulated in contemporary public discourse, class still pervades later-day British culture. Although the moral fibre of the poor has long been questioned with divisions made between the rough and respectable, traditional working class claims to dignity, hard graft and authenticity once offered a sense of worth (Charlesworth 2000). In a context where class is often dismissed as old-fashioned and irrelevant, the working class have become re-branded as 'losers'. As Walkerdine (1996) points out, class comes to be understood as part of a discourse of social mobility, with a focus on social and economic improvement. This is reflected in the way blame is readily attached to working-class mothers for failing to equip their children with the right skills for social betterment.

Class differences provoke uneasy feelings of guilt and embarrassment, making them a difficult topic to voice (Sayer 2005). While class discrimination cannot be readily justified, such inequalities are more easily defended on the grounds of merit, or moral superiority. Consequently class issues are commonly addressed through coded language and symbols that inscribe inferiority and subjectivise injustice. Without class ever being named, individuals are positioned and contained by class-specific discourses. Margaret Wetherell and Jonathon Potter (1992) describe how a similar process has occurred in relation to 'race'. Even extreme, right-wing nationalist politicians such as Jean Marie Le Pen in France are able to articulate highly racialised arguments without recourse to the morally troubling category of race. Instead, coded descriptions of primitive and advanced or superiority and inferiority map on to racial distinctions and achieve the same racist ends.

Coded representations of the working class in British culture are particularly prominent and vicious. This is illustrated by the emergence of the slang term 'chav' to ridicule and stereotype the white working classes. Sharing much in common with the American term 'trailer trash' or 'white trash', chav's are depicted as poor, ignorant, tasteless and immoral. They are presented as living in low income areas such as council estates and are marked out by specific clothes (track suits), jewellery (gaudy gold or 'bling'), brand names (Burberry) and an association with petty crime. Notably, attention is contemptuously focused on their appearance and lifestyle rather than their trade mark deprivation, with the implication being that they are to blame for their poverty. Chav's have been the butt of many jokes over the last few years, but humour barely conceals the venom driving much of this social commentary. For example, the much-cited website chavscum.com was set up to document 'Britain's peasant underclass that are taking over our towns and cities'. Many jokes forums devote whole sections to chav's, reproducing hate-saturated humour:

> Whats the similarity between a chav and a slinky?
> There's lots of fun to be had watching them fall down a steep set of stairs.

> Two chavs jump off a cliff. Who wins?
> Society.

These 'jokes' enjoy a widespread tolerance that would be hard to imagine if they were directed at any other social group. However, unlike other oppressed minorities, chav's have no claim to recognition beyond their stigmatised lifestyles, judged to be morally abject. As Alex Law argues, this is a form of class hate bolstered by humour:

> Class-based bigotry gets coded over in a way that would be disallowed by other types of social communication. Jokes acquire a transcendent quality that puts this special kind of social communication, when it is appropriately signalled to its audience as 'funny', as somehow standing outside the bounds of moral or political judgement. In this way the social damage of bigoted joking is both excused and permitted.
>
> (Law 2006)

Such representations of the working-class are highly gendered, with some of the most hateful depictions directed at women. While women are not specifically targeted, they are commonly depicted as especially repellant objects (Lawler 2005). Long before the emergence of the term 'chav', working-class women bore the brunt of the 'Essex girl' stereotype. Essex girls are now more often termed 'chavettes', and are portrayed as loud, stupid, coarse and sometimes menacing. They drink too much alcohol, wear vulgar and revealing clothes and have little self-control. Beverley Skeggs (2005) shows how such stereotypes of 'immoral, repellent' women have been reproduced of late through a media fascination with hen parties. A moral panic about an apparent rise in women's alcohol consumption has also been played out through a proliferation of images depicting drunken, raucous and sometimes unconscious working-class women. However, promiscuity is the most prominent feature of this stereotype. Portrayed as passively engaging in sex with numerous partners, often in public places, their sexual habits (alongside their appearance) are the primary focus of jokes and representations. For example, the popular British comic magazine *Viz* regularly features two characters called 'The Fat Slags' (subsequently made in to a feature film) who are obsessed with casual sex and eating. Their class location is inscribed through their strong working-class dialect, the excessive food they eat (chips) and the clothes they wear.

The promiscuity stereotype attached to working-class women is also commonly signified by the presence of babies or young children. For example, the hugely popular BBC television comedy series *Little Britain* features 'Vicky Pollard', a dim, crude schoolgirl (played by a man) who is often depicted as pregnant or wheeling a pram. Again, her working-class accent, council estate habitat and clothes unambiguously locate her in terms of class. An essential part of the humour associated with this and other representations stems from the notion that casual sex leads to casual motherhood. Children are also often used to emphasise lack of morality, with working-class mothers parodied as unhygienic and oblivious to their children's needs. In more recent years the word 'pramface' has emerged as a term of derision. Originating from the popular website *Popbitch*, the term was used to identify celebrities (often from working-class backgrounds) with a 'face better suited to pushing a pram around a housing estate'. As Angela McRobbie (2006) states, the term 'Pramface' has come to represent 'the face of impoverished, unkempt, slovenly maternity and re-stigmatised single motherhood'.

Humorous, exaggerated representations of working-class mothers are often accompanied by more serious accusations of carelessness, irresponsibility and selfishness. For example, in the late 1990s a spate of 'home alone' cases were featured in the media in which working-class mothers were exposed for leaving their children at home on their own while they went out. More recently, attention has been focused on mothers with very young, pregnant daughters. For instance, a widespread media controversy was stirred up over three schoolgirl sisters who gave birth aged 12, 14 and 16. Featured extensively in the tabloid press and in the BBC documentary *Desperate Midwives*, the family were represented as defiant and shameless. Their dependence on welfare benefits and council housing was prominently featured, prompting a crescendo of moralising summed up by the *Daily Mail* journalist Simon Heffer:

> **Shouldn't we jail the baby factory mum?**
> In some cases, the amorality of the parent gives children no chance: take the shocking case of the Atkins family of Derby, whose three girls (two underage) were pregnant by the age of 16. Their twice-divorced mother blamed the schools and Government – the consequence of a welfare state

that destroys personal responsibility. Parents can't write off their duties
in the way the atrocious Mrs Atkins did.

(Simon Heffer, *Daily Mail*, 28 May 2005)

The 'atrocious' Mrs Atkins and her pregnant daughters symbolise a 'failure'
that is individualised and extracted from a broader economic and social
context. Mrs Atkins herself was widely quoted as saying 'I don't care what
people say, I love my kids and I'm here to help them'. This was generally
taken as evidence of her brazen degeneracy, rather than an attempt by
a frightened and concerned mother to protect her vulnerable daughters.
Despite widespread and lurid coverage in the media, extreme cases like
Mrs Atkins and the more serious neglect highlighted in 'home alone' features
are highly exceptional. The implication, however, is that they are graphic
illustrations of the amorality of poor, working-class families. As such they
feed into and bolster negative stereotypes of marginalised mothers as
detached from mainstream concerns and values.

Class and race and feminism

Contemporary images of class are not just gendered, they are also heavily
racialised. Racist representations and practices are still deeply ingrained in
British society and are inextricably linked to class. Nevertheless, as culturally
constructed concepts, ethnicity, class and gender are often treated as separate
identities, attached to distinct consequences and political agendas. Early
attempts to explain inequality relied on reductionist models asserting the
primacy of economic distribution and subsuming ethnicity and gender
as manifestations of social stratification. As Floya Anthias (2005) notes, the
enduring legacy of this approach is to view class in terms of material
difference and ethnicity as a cultural phenomenon. This over-simplistic distinction obscures the way class is lived and sustained through cultural
practices, as well as the economic consequences associated with racism.

More recent approaches stress the need to develop holistic, integrated
understandings of inequality and oppression. Feminists have been at the
forefront of these debates, with black writers such as Angela Davis (1981)
and bel hooks (1989) among the first to argue for a new understanding of
gender in conjunction with race and class. During the 1970s and 1980s, gender
was often set against class as a way of understanding oppression, with many
feminists promoting a unitary view of women as a group. However, this
notion of all women sharing the same experiences as a cohesive group was
resoundingly and effectively challenged by black women, who highlighted the
issue of difference and division. As a result, feminism in the 1990s and beyond
moved towards a theorising of the differing and conflicting interests of women.
Class has come to be recognised as a crucial component shaping the way
ethnicity and gender are lived, as bell hooks eloquently explains:

Feminist theorists acknowledged the overwhelming significance of the interlocking systems of race, gender and class long before men decided to talk more about these issues together. Yet mainstream culture, particularly the mass media, was not willing to tune into a radical political discourse that was not privileging one issue over the other. Class is still often kept separate from race. And while race is often linked with gender, we still lack an ongoing collective public discourse that puts the three together in ways that illuminate for everyone how our nation is organised and what our class politics really are. Women of all races, black people of both genders are fast filling up the ranks of the poor and disenfranchised. It is in our interest to face the issue of class, to become more conscious, to know better so that we can know how best to struggle for economic justice.

(hooks 2000: 8)

bell hooks' appeal takes on greater significance in the wake of the devastation caused by hurricane Katrina when it hit the Gulf coast in the US in 2005. Natural disasters inevitably affect marginalised groups disproportionally, but the advent of Katrina brutally exposed the fused nature of class, race, ethnicity and gender. The common plight of people too poor and vulnerable to escape the disaster was displayed on television screens across the world, revealing those left behind to be predominantly black (although poor whites were also trapped), with this population made up of large numbers women with children. While class clearly distinguishes the victims of Katrina, it is fused with the injuries of race, as was highlighted by media stories with contrasting images of 'dangerous' black 'looters' with 'desperate' white 'survivors'. As Gary Younge explains:

Katrina did not create this racist image of African-Americans – it has simply laid bare its ahistorical bigotry, and in so doing exposed the lie of equal opportunity in the US. A basic understanding of human nature suggests everyone in New Orleans wanted to survive and escape. A basic understanding of American economics and history shows that, despite all the rhetoric, wealth – not hard work or personal sacrifice – is the most decisive factor in who succeeds. . . . In the Lower Ninth Ward area, which was inundated by the floodwaters, more than 98 per cent of the residents are black and more than a third live in poverty. In other words, their race and their class are so closely intertwined that to try to understand either separately is tantamount to misunderstanding both entirely.

(Younge 2005: 19)

Despite the interlocked nature of class and ethnicity, inequality is still more usually attributed to one or the other. In Britain, black and ethnic minority populations are considerably less likely to be discussed in terms of class. There is little racial ambiguity in the term 'chav', with the working classes implicitly coded as a white tribe. Tracey Reynolds (1997) suggests there is a general assumption that all black people are working class, with no need to explicitly categorise them as such. Other theorists argue that the contempt directed at the chav (often by those deemed to be 'liberals') would be difficult to sustain and justify if it included visible ethnic minorities (McRobbie 2001; Lawler 2005). In an analysis of middle-class disgust, Stephanie Lawler (2005) points out that the expulsion and exclusion of associations of white working-classness is integral to middle-class existence. The visceral emotion of disgust works to reinforce boundaries and prevent contamination.

As Ruth Frankenberg (1993) notes, 'whiteness' is a cultural space that can be experienced as amorphous and indescribable in comparison with a range of other identities marked by race, ethnicity, region, religion and class. Yet any system of differentiation impacts just as meaningfully on those it promotes as well as those it oppresses. Naming whiteness helps disrupt the unmarked, unspoken status that derives from ingrained, socially defined racial hierarchies. Over recent years a considerable body of work has emerged on this topic, seeking to define and document whiteness as an ethnicity (Byrne 2006; Back and Ware 2001; Bonnett 2000). Broadly speaking, whiteness is understood as a position of structural privilege, and as identity that embodies cultural legitimation and relative power:

> Whiteness changes over time and space and is in no way a transhistorical essence. Rather . . . it is a complexly constructed product of local, regional, national, and global relations past and present. Thus, the range of possible ways of living whiteness, for an individual white woman in a particular time and place, is delimited by the relations of racism at the moment in that place. And if whiteness varies spatially and temporarily, it is also a relational category, one that is co-constructed with a range of other racial and cultural categories, with class and with gender. This co-construction is, however, fundamentally asymmetrical, for the term whiteness signals the production and reproduction of dominance rather than subordination, normativity rather than disadvantage.
>
> (Frankenberg 1993: 236–7)

With ethnicity conceptualised as a location from which self and other is constructed, whiteness might be regarded as a system of unmarked dominant practices. Nevertheless, theorists have underlined the complexity of this process, highlighting the 'contingent hierarchy' of whiteness in terms of its intersection with class, gender and sexuality (Garner 2006). Others have pointed to the way the white working classes are constructed as a race apart. Stephanie Lawler (2005) describes a racialising move to hyper-whiten the working classes, ensuring their emblematic whiteness remains central to their continued disparagement. This represents a shift from the nineteenth-century view of the white working classes as racially 'impure', or not white enough, with the Victorian bourgeoisie associating them with non-whites, and at times constructing them as a distinct racial group (Bonnet 2000). As Lawler explains, 'now that there is at least lipservice paid to racial "diversity", and perhaps a recognition that "whiteness" itself might be troublesome, the working class becomes *too white*, embodying a racism that is officially condemned' (2005: 437). This is effectively demonstrated through Chris Haylett's (2001) analysis of UK policy discourse as saturated with representations of the white working classes as old-fashioned, backward and unable to embrace modern, multi-cultural British society.

Such depictions of the white working class also work to downplay the link between whiteness natural privilege (Skeggs 2005; Haylett 2001). At the same time, racism is constructed as a working-class problem perpetuated by 'ignorant' poor whites, effectively deflecting attention from the disproportionate and grievous inequality suffered by ethnic minorities in white middle-class-run institutions. As Beverley Skeggs argues, culture becomes the defining feature of race, with the working classes distinguished as 'dirty whites' (2005: 972). This fixation on white working-class prejudice at the expense of the arguably more powerful institutional racism associated with the middle classes also defines an emerging backlash against liberal multi-culturalism. A new social commentary has emerged to explain working-class racism on the grounds that they have been oppressed and marginalised by an emphasis on diversity at the cost of fairness and reciprocity.

According to the book *The New East End: Kinship, Race and Conflict* by the Institute for Community Studies (Dench *et al.* 2006), white east-enders express understandable resentment that the needs of Bangladeshi immigrants take precedence over rights and values of long-term residents. David Goodhart makes a similar argument, claiming that 'the left's recent love affair with diversity may come at the expense of the values and even the people that it once championed' (2004: 30). From Goodhart's perspective, Britain is becoming too diverse to sustain the sharing and solidarity that necessarily underpins generous welfare states. In this debate, the white working classes are vulnerable to being hijacked in order to represent and promote the racist sentiments of the middle-class elite. Concerns about just distribution of resources centre on issues of ethnicity, with both the white and ethnic minority working classes identified as problems, whites are portrayed as angry, backward losers, while immigrants are pathologised as insufficiently integrated freeloaders.

In the face of longstanding issues around inequality, motherhood is a site where the interactions of class, ethnicity and gender are commonly naturalised and normalised. Becoming a mother is often depicted as a destined developmental stage, constituting a primary identity for women. Crucial economic and social differences between mothers are downplayed, with emphasis placed instead on the technical applications of parenting practices and 'skills' (Gillies 2005b). As I outlined in Chapter 1, use of the gender neutral term 'parenting' disguises the fact that mothers continue to shoulder major responsibility for the day-to-day care of children. Even where gendered, the division of domestic labour is recognised; an assumption that mothers share a common bond conceals the very different experiences, choices and resources available to families depending on their class locations. Studies of ethnic-minority parenting highlight the enduring nature of structural and interpersonal racism, while also revealing the extent to which this is mediated through class (Reynolds 2005; Hill Collins 1987). As this research demonstrates, motherhood is a situated, integrated practice, with the consequences of inequality experienced emotionally as well as a materially.

Identifying and theorising the gendered politics which underpin classed experiences of motherhood requires a careful and critical consideration of the categories of identity which constitute gendered subjectivity. Feminism has traditionally sought to highlight women's experience and challenge gender inequality. However, claims made for a distinct feminist knowledge have been widely criticised for their reification of a single, universal feminist standpoint, with little consideration of other, existing marginalisations, for example black, lesbian or working-class women's perspectives (Burman 1996; hooks 1999; Stanley and Wise 1993). While most feminists recognise the risk that gender generalisations may be made at the expense of individual, contextual experience, most also oppose an exclusive focus on difference.

More specifically, the extreme relativism associated with postmodernism is regarded by many as reducing feminism to a theoretical exercise, thereby actively concealing the embedded structure of white, middle-class, male privilege. In particular, postmodern critiques of the concepts of truth and justice have been accused of paralysing practical efforts towards social progress by levelling the ethical ground on which moral judgements are made. This privileging of epistemological theory over political practice and physical experience has been criticised on theoretical as well as moral grounds. Susan Bordo (1990) has argued that a postmodern approach exchanges a positivist preoccupation with objectivity and neutrality ('a view from nowhere') for an equally problematic fantasy of protean dislocation characterised by constantly shifting viewpoints ('a dream of everywhere'). Bordo draws attention to the inescapable physical and material locatedness which works to shape and limit human thought and action:

> we are standing in concrete bodies, in a particular time and place in the 'middle' of things, always. The most sophisticated theory cannot alter this limitation on our knowledge, while too-rigid adherence to theory can make us too inflexible, too attached to a set of ideas, to freshly assess what is going on around us.
>
> (Bordo 1990: 96)

As Caroline Ramazanoglu and Janet Holland (1999) argue, while there are no straightforwardly feminist ways of knowing, feminists are able to interpret and theorise the everyday oppressive experiences of living gender. They suggest that feminists can draw on these experiences without either reifying them as essential truths about womanhood, or relativising away the grounds for political action.

Emotional dimensions of class

> In contemporary British society social class is not only etched into our culture, it is still deeply etched into our psyches.
>
> (Reay 2005a: 912)

Understandings of class are inevitably loaded with emotional meaning, although traditional theories of inequality have largely sought to suppress and rationalise such feelings to a point of virtual invisibility. As Valerie Walkerdine (1996) asserts, these models probably tell us more about middle-class projections than they do about working-class lives. A good example of this is Michael Argyle's (1994) attempt to produce a psychology of social class. During the course of his detailed analysis of social class differences, he relies implicitly on value judgements that reproduce notions of working-class inferiority. For example, in the chapter titled 'Values, sex, crime and religion' he states:

> Class differences in law breaking can be partly explained by class differences in socialisation. We show elsewhere in this book that working-class parents use more punitive discipline, are more authoritarian, have larger families, that there is less contact with fathers and that there is less use of reasoning or related methods likely to produce internalised controls.
>
> (Argyle 1994: 251)

By the end of his study, Argyle had produced a thoroughly pathologised image of the working classes. He even suggests that the higher incidence of depression found among the working classes is associated with 'less effective coping mechanisms and other aspects of personality' (1994: 292). Argyle's analysis is built on the fears, assumptions and projections from which the category of social class emerged in the first place.

Valerie Walkerdine (1996) points to similarly rationalised projections associated with Marxist accounts of class. She notes the tendency of the middle-class left to view the working classes as victims of 'false consciousness', and theorise that distorted perception prevents them from recognising and addressing their oppression. From this perspective the working classes become the focus of disappointment and contempt for their 'selfish' short-sightedness. Yet as Valerie Walkerdine suggests:

> The idea of a true as opposed to a false consciousness simply assumes a seeing or a not seeing. What if a working-class person sees and yet has myriad conscious and unconscious ways of dealing with or defending against the pains and contradictions produced out of her/his social and historical location?
>
> (Walkerdine 1996: 149)

The largely feminist-driven renaissance in class theorising is less associated with defining economic and structural characteristics and more concerned with exploring lives as they are lived and experienced. Consequently class is viewed as an affect-infused construct rather than an abstract category. In reflecting on their own working-class upbringings feminist writers like Valerie Walkerdine, Helen Lucey and Caroline Steedman laid the foundations for a new approach to class that explicitly addresses the ways in which individuals make sense of their social and economic positions in relation to others. As Diane Reay articulates, 'we need more understanding of how social class is actually lived, of how it informs our inner worlds to complement research on how it shapes our life chances in the outer world' (2005a: 913). There is increasing recognition of the interdependence of these inner and outer worlds, with studies revealing how class both produces and is produced through emotion. More specifically, theorists have explored the significance of feelings such as disgust, shame, and pride in relation to class, demonstrating how they define social relationships and practices (Gillies 2006a; Lawler 2005; Reay 2005a; Skeggs 1997, 2004).

John Kirk (2006) describes a new 'emotional politics of class' which foregrounds feelings, subjectivity and interactional dynamics. For example, Diane Reay (1995, 1997) has focused on mothers' involvement in their children's education, analysing the complex emotional and psychological consequences of living social class to show how it is central to women's attitudes, assumptions and confidences about their children's education. This area of work has also been illuminated by a focus on value systems and the moral significance of class. Andrew Sayer's (2005) book on this subject examines the moral dimension shaping interpretations of inequality, effectively showing how class informs what, how and who we value. As he demonstrates, class encompasses far more than material wealth. Class represents a framework influencing access to valued resources and relationships, and as such profoundly impacts upon our ability to lead comfortable and satisfying lives.

Despite its obvious significance, the emotional and/or moral dimension of class as it is lived and studied often goes unrecognised. Like all commentary on the subject, this book has been written from a particular emotionally invested standpoint. I write from the relatively privileged position that academia affords, having grown up in a white working-class family. I have a strong emotional connectedness to the experiences articulated in this book and a conviction that working-class mothers deserve much more than they get in terms of support, economic resources and social respect. I also believe there is an urgent need to recognise class as more than just an oppressive social construction. Class may be historically and culturally produced, but it is also recursive, in that how we are positioned or 'classified' defines our possibilities and parameters (Skeggs 1997). To ignore class is to neglect a concept that is fundamental to our choices, expectations and subjective understandings. More importantly, it would also entail dismissing the inequality and exploitation that class embodies.

A theoretical framework of class

Having underlined significance of class as a social construct with powerful consequences, I now need to explain how I have operationalised it in the context of my research. Rather than drawing on an uncritical model of structural categories of identity, I am conceptualising class as a discursive framework with real material effects. As Ian Parker states, 'discourse constructs "representations" of the world which have a reality almost as coercive as gravity' (1992: 8). The subjectivities and practices of the marginalised mothers in my study are grounded in distinct social and material positions. I would argue that these positions are generated and maintained through structured social relationships best described in terms of class. As such, it is necessary to establish a theoretical account of class, not as a fixed category, but as a fluid social and subjective location. As Diane Reay suggests:

> We need to reinvent social class as a dynamic, mobile aspect of identity that continues to permeate daily interaction.
>
> (Reay 1997: 226)

The work of the French sociologist Pierre Bourdieu has been particularly influential in informing new approaches to class. Bourdieu's complex and nuanced account of the reproduction of inequality centres on the way class is lived as an embodied subjectivity orientating individuals to the opportunities and constraints that characterise their lives. The term 'habitus' is used to refer to socialised ways of being and doing which constitute 'the internalised form of class condition and of the conditioning it entails' (Bourdieu 1979: 101). Habitus is acquired, not through conscious learning or as the result of ideological coercion, but through lived practice, and is deeply ingrained in material dispositions such as walking, talking and speaking as well as thinking and feeling. This practical habituation is described by Bourdieu as a 'second sense' or a 'feel for the game'.

It is through a combination of experience, practice and reflection that individuals develop a practical disposition to act in certain ways. As Boudieu (1977) explains, 'The habitus makes coherence and necessity out of accident and contingency' (1997: 87).

Thus, the concept of habitus represents a combination of personal and social dimensions, and is situated in time, space and place. According to Bourdieu, a dynamic dialectic characterises the integration of habitus (embodied dispositions) and 'field' (external environment). While embodied dispositions are grounded in concrete circumstance, these circumstances are shaped and transformed by the individual concerned (Reay 1995; Bourdieu 1990). Each person's habitus is singular and specific to their particular circumstances and material location, yet also consists of a collective history of family, class, gender, ethnicity etc. Criticisms of this theory have centred around reading it as a potentially mechanistic account of a passively inherited, internalised framework driving behaviour (Jenkins 1992). However, while Bourdieu emphasises the constraints and pre-dispositions that limit and shape choice, he also describes the ever-varying range of potential moves and responses that may enacted around and within structural impositions. As Diane Reay (1995) points out, Bourdieu's theory of habitus is characterised by vagueness and indeterminacy as opposed to causal laws of behaviour. As a result, the concept of habitus enables an analysis of the way language and culture constrain, shape and enable social actions.

Habitus is not just an internalised experience of class and other forms of identity, it is also characterised by access to particular kinds of social and material resources. According to Bourdieu, class can be understood in terms of 'capital movements through social space'. The configuration of this social space is stratified, with class positions determined by the arrangement of various forms of capital which can translate into power, control and influence. Bourdieu identifies four different categories of capital which are integrally interlinked. The first, 'economic capital', refers to financial assets in the form of access to money, income, inheritance etc. which determine prosperity and security. The second is 'social capital', which describes the value that can be generated from social connections through relationships or group membership. The third, 'cultural capital', is more complex in that it relates to legitimated knowledge and cultural discourses that become embodied as dispositions of the mind and body. Cultural capital can be formal, in the shape of educational qualifications, and informal, demonstrated through taste, style, deportment and social competency.

To have middle-class cultural capital is to be able to attach value to oneself through particular identifications and dis-identifications. This 'cultural game' (Bourdieu 1979) is played to the rules of an elite value system emphasising particular aesthetics and manners. Middle-class cultural capital readily converts into 'symbolic capital', the fourth key resource identified by Bourdieu. 'Symbolic capital' represents the construction the other capitals take when they are legitimated with symbolic power. For example, while certain forms of culture may be valued by the working class, only certain forms of cultural capital (middle-class forms) are legitimated by symbolic power. This constitutes what Bourdieu and Passerson (1977) termed a 'cultural arbitrary' (arbitrary in that it has no authenticity beyond its own terms of reference). Thus symbolic value is attached to activities like theatre-going, listening to classical music or reading 'challenging' novels, while watching television, playing bingo or reading magazines is denigrated. The defining of particular cultural practices and understandings as worthy or correct is viewed as act of 'symbolic violence', with the dominant imposing frameworks of meaning and value which the dominated come to accept as given. This amounts to 'misrecognition', a process by which power relations are not recognised as such, but are instead viewed in terms which make them seem legitimate and unquestionable.

In their discussion of symbolic violence, Bourdieu and Passeron (1977) argue that knowledge and learning are not neutral practices. They emphasise the role of schools and other institutions as agents of cultural enforcement, thereby reproducing power relations. From this perspective, working-class children are likely to experience conflict between their situated cultural knowledge and the sanctioned, middle-class knowledge they encounter in the classroom. However, they are socialised to view their own struggles and the success of their middle-class peers as evidence of their own inferior ability verses their class mates' superior potential. With educational progress presented in terms of hard work and natural intelligence, class inequality is effectively obscured.

To summarise then, social space is stratified in terms of key resources (economic, social, cultural and symbolic capital). Individuals are born into a designated social space which is defined by access to capitals, but capitals are also tied to social positions in that being black, working-class and a woman provides limited access. As Skeggs explains:

> The social relations of capitals into which we are born and move have been constructed historically through struggles over assets and space. Gender, class and race are not capitals as such, rather they provide the relations in which capitals come to be organised and valued.
>
> (Skeggs 1997: 9)

The amount and type of capitals an individual possesses, and gains or looses over time, determines both their position within the social space at any one time, as well as their overall trajectory. An advantage of Bourdieu's 'metaphors of capital' is that class can be theorised as a social construction that has concrete effects on the lives of those who are contained by it. Class positions can be seen as institutionalised by the legitimation of certain forms of culture. The inability to convert cultural capital into symbolic capital severely restricts and contains access to other forms of capital, and as a result inequalities are maintained and reproduced. In this sense class inequalities can be conceptualised in terms of multiple axis, each relating to different forms of capital (Sayer 2005).

Beverley Skeggs (1997) also distinguishes between the different fields in which capitals are traded on. Local arenas use different criteria to legitimise in comparison to national or global arenas. She notes how in some working-class areas *not* being middle class is valued, like the macho physicality identified by Willis (1977) in his study of working-class males. However, these different arenas have very different powers in that the working classes have no institutional sites to assert their legitimacy. Structures built around the law, education, health and the media devalue local working-class cultural worth and confine its value in wider capital arenas. This leads to a restriction of movement through the social space. The experience of constraint and limited power is fundamental to the construction of the individual habitus. Structural and social relations generate the internalised framework that shapes the availability and appropriateness of practices, subject positions and cultural values.

There are, then, a number of ways in which I theorise class in this book. First, the mothers I have interviewed have been defined as working class in terms of their limited access to capitals and restricted movement in social space. Second, class is understood as a construct that has very real effects on women's lives, and as part of a discourse which pathologises and dis-empowers working-class mothers in particular. Being working class means being positioned by categorisations and representations that actively uphold and maintain structural inequalities. Third, class, as a form of material positioning, is viewed as central to the subjectivity (or habitus) of working-class mothers.

Studying working-class mothers

As Beverely Skeggs (1997) points out, it is important to create discursive space in order to ensure that experiences are not ignored because those with power do not recognise them. Yet studies of parenting often overlook key constraints and resources and focus on themes and practices generalised across social groups. As a result, understandings and perspectives may be interpreted as culturally or socially defined reference points, rather than materially grounded frameworks of meaning. This book represents a detailed and contextualised exploration of individual accounts in order to draw out the crucial significance of class. While I am aware that I might be accused of invoking deterministic notions by emphasising the relevance of situated, material factors to the lives of mothers, I am anxious to avoid locating this analysis within the confines of a conventional 'agency/structure' debate. Instead I have tried to transcend the dualistic framework of such debates to locate agency within its concrete materiality. Like Susan Bordo (1998), I have sought to 'bring body to theory', to show how the physical, material, cultural, social and personal are merged, producing particular situations and experiences. As Bordo explains:

> 'Materiality', in the broadest terms, signifies for me our finitude. It refers to our inescapable physical locatedness in time and space, in history and culture, both of which not only shape us . . . but also limit us.
>
> (Bordo 1998: 90)

Bourdieu's concept of 'habitus' best captures this complex dynamic of personal agency and material positioning. Drawing on this methodological approach allows agency and structure to be reconciled without constructing the individual and society as separate entities. The choices and actions of the mothers in this study can be viewed in terms of the dialectical relationship between habitus and field (or location). Close analysis of the mothers' accounts show how each woman's unique circumstances generate a range of potential opportunities within similar, structurally confined boundaries. But the choices and freedom available to these women are contained within an internalised framework or 'habitus', which makes some possibilities distinctly less conceivable than others.

Highlighting the corporeal, material context shaping individual lives and experiences allows a more integrated approach to the study of inequality. From this perspective oppression can be see in terms of interconnected determinants including class, race, ethnicity, gender and sexuality. As Floya Anthias (2005) argues, it is important to recognise these social divisions as cross-cutting and mutually reinforcing, rather than interconnected but distinct. This allows exploration of the 'multiple, uneven and contradictory social patterns of domination and subordination' (Anthias 2005: 37). Rather than identifying universal commonalities which constitute women's identities and experiences as working-class mothers, I have sought to demonstrate how class, gender and ethnicity is produced and lived in specific situations.

Treating a concept like social class as if it existed in some kind of objective, independent realm is problematic in that it limits understanding of the way oppression and inequality are actually experienced. Nevertheless, some form of abstract theorising is necessary in order to understand and change material and social relationships. As Ian Parker points out, the reification of certain discourses performs the crucial function of enabling a more effective exploration of power networks:

> Discourses provide frameworks for debating the value of one way of talking about reality over other ways. . . . Discourse analysis deliberately systematises different ways of talking so we can understand them better.
>
> (Parker 1992: 5)

From this perspective we need to be able to draw on wider discourses like social class in order to understand their real effects. The distinction drawn throughout the book between the working and middle classes is essentially pragmatic, with this categorisation inevitably overlaying much greater complexity. As I have stated, the mothers featured in this book are classed on the basis of their access to Bourdieu's core capitals. I will show in the next chapter that all had low incomes, lacked formal educational qualifications, and lived and socialised in disadvantaged communities. Categorising them in this way allows analysis of the real effects of class as a set of system-ised social relationships with powerful material consequences, while still preserving space to explore the diverse way it is actually lived.

Chapter 3

Mothering and material struggle

As I outlined in the previous chapter, class constitutes far more than an economic relationship. Nevertheless, at a fundamental level, lifestyles and opportunities are tied to an everyday material reality. In this chapter I will outline the kinds of disadvantage faced by the mothers in the sample and explore how they cope on a day-by-day basis. I will begin by examining the wider context in which poor mothers in the UK raise their children by providing a brief picture of low-income Britain. I will then highlight some more personal stories of getting by from the mothers in the sample. These accounts show how obtaining sufficient money and securing decent housing are consuming imperatives, shaping biographies and experiences of mother-hood. By focusing on specific examples the chapter will explore the meaning of raising children in the context of struggling to survive with very little money, power or security. Alongside various stories and experiences from mothers in the sample are three more detailed accounts: the first tells of life as a lone mother on benefits; the second documents the experiences of a re-partnered mother and step-mother; the third examines the life of a 'working poor' family through the eyes of a migrant wife and mother. These stories detail the very particular challenges faced by three women, but they also serve to illustrate themes shared across the whole sample, such as vulnerability, deprivation, injustice, determination, commitment and resourcefulness.

Poverty and inequality in the UK

While there is much debate about the definitions and causes of poverty, there is general agreement that it constitutes a serious problem in contemporary Britain. A standard measure involves a 'poverty line', set at 60 per cent of median income, below which individuals and families are regarded as income poor. According to the Child Poverty Action Group in 2003/4, 21 per cent of people in the UK are living below this line, a rise from 13 per cent in 1979. This figure increases to 26 per cent if poverty is defined as lacking two or more 'socially perceived necessities' because they cannot be afforded (Flaherty *et al.* 2004). These include basic needs like a warm coat or shoes. Families are particularly vulnerable to poverty, with 52 per cent of all income-poor being comprised of households containing a child. Lone-parent families face the greatest risk of hardship, with single parents two and a half times more likely to be surviving on a low income than couples with children (Palmer *et al.* 2005). Black and minority ethnic groups in the UK are also disproportionately affected, with more than half the children of Pakistani, Bangladeshi and Black parents living in poverty (Department for Work and Pensions 2005).

Research confirms the bleak reality of life in Britain as experienced by the substantial number of mothers and their children living on low incomes. A recent study found that that half of parents on a low income go hungry in order to feed someone else in the family, while around 100,000 families are currently estimated to be homeless (Shelter 2004b). Coping with this kind deprivation has a significant impact on life chances. Poor children are more likely to weigh less at birth and are twice as likely to die before their first birthday compared to those in better-off families. They are also twice as likely to develop physical and mental illness, and have a significantly lower life expectancy. Children from poor families are similarly disadvantaged when it comes to education. They are less likely to gain qualifications than children from average income families, and have a higher risk of being excluded from school (Palmer *et al.* 2005). As many campaigning organisations have pointed out, poverty is not just about levels of income. It is a relative concept that raises crucial questions about social justice. While a welfare safety net in the UK prevents most poor people from starving, those on low incomes have a low quality of life that excludes them from activities and material goods others take for granted. Living standards and incomes in the UK have grown steadily over the years, but these gains have been far from equally distributed. The gap between the rich and poor in Britain grew dramatically in the 1980s, and the income of the top 1 per cent continues to rise (Institute for Fiscal Studies 2006).

In the context of these unprecedented levels of inequality, policy-makers in the UK espouse a US-inspired conviction that paid work is the only acceptable answer to poverty. Dependence on the state for direct financial support is seen as problematic, and instead the government prefers to see itself as responsible for generating resources and opportunities to help citizens to contribute the moral economy (Gray 2004; Dwyer 2002). Welfare reform in the UK has focused on tightening access to state support and promoting tax credits as an alternative means-tested benefit. These credits can be claimed direct from the government by low-paid workers. Although they have raised the living standards of many families in work, in practice they represent a government subsidy to low-paying employers. This state top-up for low wages quenches a growing demand for a more 'flexible' workforce in Europe, ensuring that the poor and most vulnerable are forced into badly paid, non-unionised, temporary and part-time jobs. In an analysis of European welfare developments, Anne Gray (2004) describes this trend as 'flexplotation' and shows how the UK is moving to a system resembling American 'workfare', where state benefits are made dependent on participation training or work that is often menial and labour-intensive.

In the UK poverty is now almost exclusively discussed in relation to worklessness rather than low income, and there is very little consideration of the role of state benefits in alleviating hardship. Yet, as this chapter will demonstrate, paid work is not always a feasible or reasonable option for parents. Even where paid employment is a desirable outcome, issues of social justice and inequality cannot be ignored. For many, a regular wage is not enough to secure a reasonable standard of living. In 2005, 4½ million adults in the UK aged 22 to retirement were paid less than £6.50 per hour. Two-thirds of these were women and a half were part-time workers (New Policy Institute 2006). The consequences of treating employment as the only solution to poverty are most evident in America, where large numbers of 'working-poor' families often struggle to meet basic needs. A range of studies have documented the extent of deprivation suffered by those officially classified as above the poverty threshold but reliant on poorly paid, insecure jobs (Allegretto 2005; Shulman 2003; Shirk et al. 1999). Accessing and maintaining a safe, decent standard of living continues to be a challenge for those pushed to the margins of UK society, as the experiences of the mothers in this book confirm.

Making ends meet: parenting on a low income

The struggle to achieve some financial security on a low income is a feature of all the mothers' accounts. Material considerations or necessities were at the heart of many basic choices and were the source of much anxiety and effort. All the mothers worked hard to survive on the little money they received either from paid employment, welfare benefits or their partners. Decisions about whether to seek paid employment or care full time for their children were not taken lightly, and were heavily dependent on levels of investment in and involvement with male partners. As Simon Duncan and Ros Edwards (1999, 2003) reveal in a study of lone mothers, understandings of what constitutes good parenting are shaped by distinct 'gendered moral rationalities'. Judgments about whether or how to combine paid employment with unpaid childcare depend on norms, values and beliefs as well as economic need.

For example, some mothers prioritised being at home for their children above any extra money they might earn from working, although this was inevitably contextualised by the opportunities and constraints facing them. Employment options were for the most part limited to low paid, insecure posts that could be fitted around childcare responsibilities. Paying a stranger to look after your children in order to work full time was viewed as morally dubious by number of the mothers. From their perspective, parenting is in itself is a full-time responsibility that must be prioritised above financial constraints. Furthermore, many of these mothers had also taken on unpaid caring responsibilities in the community. For example, Denise looks after her recently bereaved father and two elderly neighbours in her street, and Julie provides free childcare to allow her sister work. In Chapter 4 I show how this invisible labour reflects a more relational connected sense of self, and explore the moral value these women attach to mothering in more detail in Chapter 6, but for now it is important to note the contrast between the commitments made by these women and the prevailing image of the thoughtless, selfish working-class mother I outlined in the first two chapters.

Those who took on full-time employment were also driven by their perception of what was best for their children. Pros and cons were carefully weighed up, and a number of factors were taken into consideration. For some, bringing in more money was crucial in order to enable day-to-day survival. For example, Annette works full time during the week as a receptionist, but in the light of her mounting debt feels she needs to start working Saturdays as well. Other mothers worked to save money for specific purposes. Sam took on a temporary job delivering leaflets so that she could take her children on a holiday, while Meena and her husband work unfeasibly long hours in an attempt to save a deposit that would allow them to buy their council flat. For other mothers, working was viewed as an investment that would pay off in the long term. For example, Louise explained how she returned to work soon after having her two children even though she was initially worse off financially:

> Yeah yeah, I felt really bad because here I was bringing two kids into the world and I couldn't give them anything that I wanted to give them. And I thought, you know, what am I doing? So it's up to me to make the change so I decided to, you know, give them to a child minder, and go back to work so I could, and that's what I did. I gave her all my wages, and more just so that I could go back to work, so that when they'd be at school I'd already be in a job and then I'd reap some benefit from it.

In Louise's case she was able to make this initial financial loss because she had a partner in full-time employment. For other parents, like Paula and her husband, a dual income was possible because employment was home based and flexible, allowing childcare responsibilities to be met. However, full-time work for the mothers in this sample invariably involved long hours and low pay. For some of the mothers, this was simply not a viable way of meeting financial needs and as a result they were forced to live on state benefits. For example, Naomi recently fled Sudan as a refugee with her husband and two daughters. Although the family has now been granted indefinite leave to remain in the UK, they rely on sickness benefits to get by. Naomi's English is poor and her husband, Daniel, has serious heart problems and a bad back. The family are living in temporary council accommodation in a deprived inner-city area where both Naomi and Daniel have both been the victims of street crime and burglary. Their temporary housing status requires them to be prepared to pack up and move at short notice, and this has already happened once before. There is little prospect of Naomi finding appropriate paid employment, and even if an opportunity arose, her first concern is to ensure that she remains available for her children. She feels a strong duty to provide stability, help the children overcome their traumatic past experiences, and protect them from the violent crime and drug culture that currently surrounds them. Notably, Naomi is the only partnered mother in the sample dependent on state benefits. Lone mothers are considerably more likely to rely on welfare, and as a result they are particularly vulnerable to financial hardship.

Lone mothers and the state

Despite a pervasive liberal rhetoric in the UK acknowledging and embracing increasing plurality and diversity in family forms, public and political concern still coalesces around family breakdown in terms of the cost to the exchequer and the consequences for children. Lone mothers who draw state benefits crystallise this anxiety, drawing reactions that range from fury to sympathy. Simon Duncan and Ros Edwards (1999) highlighted the recurrent demonisation of lone mothers that occurred in the UK through the 1980s and 1990s, characterised by accusations of benefit scrounging and rearing delinquent children. Although there have always been concerns about the moral character of the poor, New Right critiques explicitly accused welfare benefit systems of precipitating a breakdown in family life and social values. This moral panic was reflected in increasingly harsh rhetoric about selfish, callous women who were getting pregnant just to secure council flats.

This vilification of lone mothers was softened in the late 1990s by the incoming Labour government in the UK, but the moral undertone lingers. Heterosexual marriage is still promoted as the best option for children within a more general recognition of the proliferation of alternative family forms. Statistics are regularly cited to highlight the disadvantage faced by children of lone mothers, suggesting they are less likely to gain qualifications and are more likely to grow up suffering poor health and unemployment (Civitas 2002). However, statistics also show the severe deprivation associated with raising children alone. Lone parents are amongst the poorest groups in society and are often forced to rely on megre state benefits (Palmer *et al.* 2005). This link between poverty and lone parenting is generally acknowledged, but more often than not it is the status of lone motherhood, as opposed to the vulnerability to poverty, that is problematised.

Government efforts to tackle lone-parent poverty reflect a more general lack of acknowledgement of the full-time and demanding task of raising children. In contradiction to the contemporary preoccupation with parenting skills, the acceptability of lone motherhood is more often evaluated through economic status rather than parenting practices or commitment. While financially independent lone parents are generally tolerated, mothers who rely on state benefits remain the object of public consternation. Commonly represented as a drain on the public purse and a threat to stability and social order, such mothers have found themselves the focus of a UK government target to ensure that 70 per cent are in paid employment by 2010 (Treasury 2000). Lone parents drawing welfare benefits are now obliged to receive advice on how they might get a job, regardless of whether they feel they already have one. As some social commentators have noted, this logic could result in a chain of lone mothers each employed to care for the other's children. Yet the option of raising benefit entitlements to remove the burden of poverty and support parents who wish to act as full-time carers is met with morally founded objections. A determination to avoid encouraging lone motherhood as a lifestyle 'choice', combined with a more general male-orientated valorisation of participation in the labour market, sustains an essentially blaming view of welfare recipients as lazy, irresponsible and indifferent to the needs of their children. This summed up by Frank Field, a prominent British labour politician and campaigner for welfare reform, who argues that state benefits should be based on a contract and removed along with children if necessary:

> Children are snatching food off the table because they're so hungry. Some parents do not have any idea of their responsibilities and I do not believe that children should be brought up in these conditions. Whereas in the past we've been too free in hoovering up children into care, there is clearly a need for some children to be fostered rather than to be so hurt and damaged by the behaviour of their parents as they are at present. The remedial work we now have to do is to give a semblance of order to children's lives. The intervention at the end of the day, when all else has failed, has to be fundamental. The primary purpose is to service the needs of the children and in the most extreme cases – for their own welfare – they must be taken away, I think, until the parent learns to behave. The children should not grow up thinking this is normal behaviour.
>
> (Frank Field, interview with Paul Dornan 2004: 117)

Detailed examination of the lives, experiences and values of parents on benefits reveal a very different picture. This up-close approach is enormously useful for understanding specific decisions and constraints, and for gaining a broader appreciation of how life events unfold and develop. In-depth analysis of accounts from the lone mothers in this book who are in receipt of welfare benefits highlights the skewed nature of current policy debates. These women's lives are characterised by severe hardship and adversity which was certainly not of their own choosing or making. Instead they cope with deprivation as part of their determination to make a better life for their children. Although bringing up a child alone is a perfectly valid option, the lone mothers featured in this book would, if they had the choice, have preferred to parent with a supportive partner. This was simply not an option, given their need to deal constructively with violent, undermining or absent fathers. Drawing benefits gave them the financial independence enabling them to break away from unworkable family ties that were often damaging, and sometimes extremely dangerous for their children. If these mothers had walked away from their responsibilities (as their partners did in many cases) they would have faced a considerably brighter financial future. Yet they stayed and actively struggled to make the best of the resources available to them. This meant sheltering, feeding, clothing and schooling children on an income barely sufficient to sustain one individual, while actively compensating for the day-to-day experience of disadvantage through love, protection and humour and affirmation.

Lone mothering on welfare benefits – Sam's story

Sam is a lone mother financially reliant on welfare benefits. Her account of how she came to be in this situation and how she and her two children get by provides a much-needed insight into to the real experience of material disadvantage so commonly associated with lone parenthood. Her story also highlights the less visible levels of resilience and determination characteristic of all the marginalised mothers featured in this book.

Sam has brought her two children up on her own for two and a half years. She met the children's father, Kevin, when she left school, and soon after decided she wanted to have his baby. At the time Kevin was working as a builder, while Sam worked in a local shop. While their incomes were not high, money was not a particular worry. They moved into a friend's flat together, and Sophie (now 6) was finally born after two miscarriages. Sam stressed how desperately she wanted a baby, and emphasised the joyful and happy reactions she received from friends and family. Although Sam had initially intended to parent with Kevin, their relationship deteriorated significantly after their daughter was born. Their friend needed his flat back and they were forced to move in with Kevin's parents while they waited for a council tenancy. This was a difficult period marked by a lack of space and privacy. Kevin's behaviour added to this pressure. Sam explained how her pregnancy seemed to mark a real change in Kevin, prompting him to become complacent and uncaring. Securing their own council flat eased the pressure a bit, but according to Sam, Kevin remained emotionally distant and uninvolved in child care.

Shortly after Sophie was born, Kevin lost his job as a builder and started working as a ticket tout at large sports events and concerts. Unbeknown at the time to Sam, he also began dealing in and consuming large quantities of drugs, cocaine in particular. He would disappear for days on end, and when he did spend time at home his behaviour was erratic and often abusive. Sam described how, as Kevin's drug habit worsened, he became increasingly unreasonable and bad tempered. Her desperate attempts to help him give up the cocaine had just led to increasingly furious arguments. Sam was caring for Sophie full time and was financially reliant on Kevin, but he seemed to become resentful of this and often 'forgot' to bring money home. Sam expressed the anger and despair she felt when he stole money her parents had given to Sophie, and how he reacted violently when she challenged him about it. According to Sam, cocaine had turned Kevin into a 'psycho', incapable of considering the needs of his child. She decided enough was enough shortly after a distressing row, in which Kevin's anger had spiralled out of control and he had stabbed her in the head with a fork. She sought legal advice to have Kevin evicted, and called the police when he tried to get back into the flat. She also applied to the council to re-house herself and Sophie some distance away from him, describing this move as 'cutting off'.

Sam's decision to throw Kevin out and build a new, safe life for herself and Sophie was driven by her evaluation of daughter's best interests. It took particular courage, not just to deal with Kevin's violent and intimidating behaviour, but also to face the prospect of raising her daughter alone. She described how one particular incident steeled her resolve to make this change, for Sophie's sake:

One time she actually run into the kitchen and peed herself, because she was so scared of us two fighting. And that's the time when I thought to myself, right, you got to stop now. So that's when I ended up contacting the solicitor.

You weren't married though?

No, I wasn't married.

So why did you contact the solicitor, was it to . . .?

Just to chuck Kevin out. Get him out. And so that's what I done. And I, um, during that time, he didn't know I'd done that. But during that time he ended up going mad and I had to call the police on him . . . Mmh, it was, it was very horrible at the time because I thought, oh now I've got to bring up this baby on my own. And I was only young, well I was young-minded. I was like 20, 21 and I was very youngish-minded. Do you know what I mean, like? Like I'm, I always had to have someone to rely on. And Kevin there, I'm relying on him and he just wasn't there for me like, he was just doing what he wanted to do. So she did, she suffered. Sophie suffered. But when we moved away she become more relaxed and as time went on she was more, I mean she's so confident now. I mean she's really good. She's really come a long way since then.

Sophie wetting herself through fear was the final straw for Sam, provoking her to take what was clearly a psychologically daunting step. While Kevin was making life unbearable for them, deciding to give up on him and go it alone was far from easy. Sam was forced to navigate a maze of practical and material challenges before she and Sophie could feel safe and able to face the future. This meant taking legal steps to protect herself and her daughter by obtaining a court order, and then persuading council officials to re-house them in a decent property. It took much determination and persistence on Sam's part to organise the transfer. The first accomodation Sam was offered was barely habitable and in area she regarded as positively dangerous. After much anxious deliberation she felt she had little choice but to turn it down. She felt strongly that Sophie needed somewhere safe to recover from the trauma of the previous few years. Shortly after she was offered a small two-bedroom house on a purpose-built estate. It was tatty and in need or redecoration, but Sam jumped at this opportunity and they moved in as soon as they could. Furnishing and redecorating has been a slow process due to lack of money, but for Sam the house represents a haven of safety and security.

Reflecting back, Sam views her decision to break up with Kevin as a turning point that led her to become stronger and more assertive. Discussing the emotional turmoil she experienced at this time, she explained how she was forced to take action when she was 'young-minded', subjugated and unsure of her ability to cope alone. For Sam, becoming lone mother marked a subjective change from a vulnerable, dependant 'child' to an assertive, independent 'adult'. Although Sam's decision is presented as less of a choice and more of a necessary adaptation, the significance of this change for herself and her child is fundamental to her account of motherhood. Her determination to build a new independent family comprised of herself and her daughter increased her confidence and provided her with a strong sense of achievement. This was dampened, however, by the day-by-day grind of managing on next to no money and often having to go without things that other people would consider essential. Sam obtained a social security loan to buy some basic things for the house, but was constantly worried about keeping Sophie in shoes, coats and the toys Sam felt she deserved. Moving away from her home with Kevin entailed leaving behind a network of family and friends she would ordinarily have turned to for support. Sam's development from a young-minded, reliant person to an independent, assertive single mother was essential, not only to make the move in the first place, but also to sustain such a demanding lifestyle.

For over a year neither Sam nor Sophie had any contact with Kevin, who during this period had been able to overcome his drug problem and start working again. Eventually, after Kevin had made contact with her mother, Sam allowed him to visit the new house, and to see Sophie regularly. This decision to re-establish a relationship with Kevin was taken in the context of Sam having built a new reserve of personal strength and confidence and Kevin seeming to have recovered almost to his old self. Sam explained that although there was no official reunion between herself and Kevin during this time, they slept together on several occasions. As she stated, 'We wasn't together, we was just having sex together'. From Sam's perspective, this lack of emotional involvement was indicative of her newly gained independence and self-reliance. She emphasised how falling pregnant for the second time was a big shock for both of them. Initially Kevin refused to believe the baby was his, even though Sam had not been seeing anyone else. Faced with Kevin's hostile reaction and her personal fears and uncertainties, Sam went to the doctor and requested an abortion. She got as far as lying on the trolley to be wheeled to the operating theatre before she changed her mind. Sam walked out of the hospital with a clear intention to have the baby and a renewed determination to look after both her children on her own.

Falling pregnant with Joe and deciding to keep him was viewed by Sam as a highly significant turning point in her life. She described how walking out of the abortion clinic at the last minute had felt empowering, because the decision to have another child as a lone mother had been made on her own terms:

> It was good that I went through it all, 'cos now I know my definite decision was to have had him.

While Sam is clearly proud of her ability to cope, she does acknowledge the stresses and strains that characterise her life, if only to dismiss them as unavoidable. She describes herself as a 'loner', and emphasises a lack of dependence when discussing relationships with anyone other than her children. Her account reveals the limited resources she is able to access in the course of bringing her children up and her precarious isolation. Her description of her life with the children after she moved was conspicuously different from her previous focus on the fuss and attention she had received from friends and family after Sophie had been born. For example, she described the different experience of giving birth to Joe while Kevin stood away from her.

I was pregnant with Joe and gave birth to him on my front room floor.

Oh no!

Yeah.

How did that happen then?

Um, he was 20 minutes and I had about 20 men around me while I was giving birth.

Who were they then?

All the paediatricians and the ambulance men and, and they were all telling me not to push and I'm saying I've got to push. And I was just crawling around the floor saying ohhh it hurts, it hurts . . . Kevin was on the sofa and all he did was poo himself 'cos he didn't know what to do.

[Laughs]

He was just like, not literally but he was like, oh I've got to go out and have a fag. He weren't no help at all, whereas with Sophie he was a lot of help.

Oh he, was he?

Yeah.

How did he help then, was he there at the birth?

He was there at the birth, and I completely wrecked his shirt. He was being there and saying push, go on and it was really good. But when I gave birth to Joe he stood away from me, he was sitting on the settee like. And he went white, and they were more interested in him than they were in me like. And I'm going through all this pain. And then, um [laughs] then when Kevin phoned the ambulance, um 999, what did he say. I said, well, I said you've got to phone the ambulance 'cos I've broke me waters. So he turned round and said what's the number?

Oh [laughs].

I said 999 like you stupid sod. So he phoned the ambulance and then he was on the phone to the ambulance lady and, um, and the lady said turn the fire on, so he turned round and said don't think she's having it here 'cos she's not, like. And the lady said yes she is, she's having it there, sort of thing.

While this experience is described with humour, the primary focus of this story is the lack of support she received in this emergency situation. The contrast between Kevin's active participation in Sophie's birth and his distanced, reluctant involvement in Joe's birth was accepted by Sam as a consequence of her move to independence. Shortly after Joe (now 2½) was born, Kevin announced that he had got himself a building job in China and that he would be gone for eight months. Much to Sam's anger, Kevin made no attempt to contact his children during this time and he even forgot Sophie's birthday. He arrived back a year later with a new Chinese wife and a desire to start seeing both children regularly again. Sam agreed, reluctantly and warily, having seen the distress Sophie went through when her father disappeared without a word for a year. He now sees both children relatively regularly and contributes a small amount of money to the children's upbringing.

The bleak necessity of coping alone with little resources or support is a significant feature of Sam's account of life with her children. Financially she gets by on a day-by-day basis. When things get particularly tight or money is needed for something specific, she takes a risk and supplements her benefits with cash-in-hand work. From time to time she takes on the poorly paid and physically demanding job of delivering leaflets during the day, while worrying constantly that she might be caught. For Sam, the price of autonomy and security as a single mother is accepting full responsibility and accountability for the welfare of her children, and this inevitably takes a heavy toll. Her perceived duty to remain contained and in control eventually led to a short but serious mental breakdown. Having reached a level of exhaustion, she was forced to recognise her vulnerability and limitations:

> Well they said it was, they, um, how did they put it, seven years of stress built up. There was four people in my family that died.
>
> Oh god really, how awful.
>
> Yeah, um, there was, then there was Sophie, then I had, this isn't in order what I'm telling you, this is all in the seven years.
>
> Right.
>
> Then I had to bring a baby up on my own . . . Yeah, then I found out that Kevin had got married and then it, er, also it was because I didn't have my own place when we were together and we had to live with his mum. Then it was the new house, there was about 12 things and at the end of it my niece had died in a premature birth, so that was the end, that was the break. So then I got took into hospital. Well, I didn't actually get taken, I was, they voluntarily admitted me. They said you're cracking up and they admitted me for two weeks in a mental hospital and they said just rest . . .
>
> Who looked after the kids then?
>
> Um, Kevin and, um [his wife] had the kids for two weeks and all I did was sleep eat, sleep eat, sleep eat . . . they said it's where I was coping with so much on my own and, um, everybody thought, genuinely they all thought I was a strong, strong person and I could cope and I could do this and I could do that. And then, and even now my mum says why didn't you tell us, why didn't you tell us you were going through a hard time? But it wasn't, I coped with it, that's how I was coping. I thought that I was OK.
>
> So it was just overload.

Yeah, it was. That's what they said, 'cos I couldn't come up for air. Then keep having these stresses and stresses and it just pushed me right down to the end [pause] but I was glad I went to hospital 'cos I had a rest and I sorted a lot out in my mind as well. . . . Yeah, I was in there for two weeks. Two whole weeks and there was all these mental patients round me and I thought, I'm not like that, I just need a rest. And I said to him, he said to me I'm going to admit you for two weeks and I said, WHAT? like and he said, I'll admit you for two weeks and I said, oh I can't go to a mental hospital, I'm not mental. He said no you need the rest, you need the rest. I said I'm normal, I'm normal and he said what's normal . . . Yeah, it was like, what's normal? So he said that's why I'm going to admit you to rest for two. So that's when they admitted me and my whole family was shocked, you know. They didn't believe it, they thought that I was coping with everything and I weren't. I weren't coping with nothing. I couldn't cope. But now my mum knows, do you know, if I went round there and said look mum blah blah blah blah blah, now she knows that to help, whereas before I didn't used to ask for it.

Right, so people are a bit more aware now that you need a bit more?

Even myself.

Yeah, that's something as well.

I know how far to go down before to ask for . . .

Yeah, I suppose in a way, that's good in that sense, I suppose at least you know now.

Oh yeah, it's done me a favour having the breakdown, it really has. I know it sounds weird, but it's done me a favour. Because where I was going, so low down I touched bottom and felt fucking hell, that was bottom and then now I'm like rebuilding myself back up again and it's done me a right favour because now people know that I'm only human and I'm always, um, can't cope with everything

Sam described how her attempts to cope in the face of continuous, mounting stress produced a convincing performance, persuading even herself that she was getting by. The experience of confusion and her inability to recognise her own limit of endurance is a prominent feature of her account of her breakdown, along with a passive, distanced description of what actually happened to her. The term 'breakdown' in itself suggests that she reached a point at which she stopped functioning, rather like a piece of machinery. The distinction Sam makes between non-functioning and malfunctioning appears to be an important one for her. According to Sam, the shocked reaction of her family to her being hospitalised was shared by Sam herself, but her ability to separate herself as someone who 'just needs a rest' from the other 'mental patients' enables her to view the two weeks as a necessary recuperation period. Sam's life has changed very little since the breakdown, and she continues to draw on extraordinary personal reserves in her struggle to get by and fulfil her definition of a good mother.

The other lone mothers in the sample, and their children, faced similar material challenges to Sam. Sarah (discussed in Chapter 4) described how lack of money and cramped, temporary housing conditions severely constrained her role as a mother, preventing her caring full time for her daughter for a period. Julie (discussed in Chapter 5) lives on a crime-ridden estate and relies on financial and practical support from a tight-knit but demanding network of family and friends. Surviving on state benefits stretches these women's resilience to the limits, but lone mothers in paid work also struggled to make ends meet, often coping with poor housing, financial insecurity and debt. For example, when Annette's partner left her with two children and a mass of unpaid bills she sank further into debt, which she is still paying off three years later:

> When I first split up with the children's dad, because we had a lot of debts and at the time he was always the one, even though we were both working, he was always the one who always paid bills, so I had no idea about coping with bills or managing my money. I was taking a lot of things out on credit, because of having to pay these bills that he left me with. So in the end it was like a never ending story and we had to live on things like cereal or oven chips for a while until the money started picking up again.

A recent fire, caused when her daughter left a candle unattended, compounded this financial pressure. With money so tight, Annette had not been able to afford insurance and the housing association are charging her £1,000 for the damage. Annette also needs to find the money to redecorate, replace the curtains and the damaged bedside cabinet. As Sam's story highlights, the economic and emotional strain of caring for children alone is to a certain extent compensated by increased confidence and personal control, and this was much appreciated by mothers who had suffered abusive or destabilising partners. Sam was particularly determined not to give up her autonomy:

> And I think to myself, well, I don't want another man living with me [laughs] and spoiling what I've actually earned, and what I've bought. I mean, I've made these curtains and everything like with the help of my Mum.

Re-making families: investing in a man

While Sam fiercely guards her independence, other mothers in the sample were more willing to trade in self-sufficiency by investing in new personal relationships and creating stepfamilies. Public representations of lone mothers are often tempered by an expectation that their status is transient, an interlude between 'normal' heterosexual coupledom (Alldred 1996). Stepfamilies, however, occupy a contradictory location, embodying both danger and a potential path to respectability. The association between step-parenting and sexual, physical and emotional child abuse is culturally ingrained, and reinforced by media horror stories and evolutionary rationalisations, stressing the primacy of biological ties. For example, in Martin Daly and Margo Wilson's (1999) book *The Truth About Cinderella* it is argued that stepchildren are at a higher risk of abuse and neglect. This evolutionary theory glosses over the fact that such cases constitute a minority of stepfamily households, and can give no explanation as to why children are still more likely to experience abuse at the hands of a biological parent (Turney 1999).

Yet if stepfamilies are closely modelled on the conventional nuclear family with a working father, re-partnering for lone mothers is interpreted as an attempt to provide a more 'secure' environment in which to raise a child. Thus step-parents who conform to nuclear family conventions may be constructed within the margins of normativity. Although in the context of overwhelmingly negative connotations attached to stepfamily life, this representation can be dependent on achieving reconstitution until the 'seams' no longer show. As a study of parenting and step-parenting after divorce and separation found, few parents are comfortable with the term 'stepfamily', with most feeling the word did not adequately describe their circumstances or their experience (Ribbens McCarthy *et al.* 2003).

Positive discourses surrounding step-parenting are virtually non-existent, possibly because stepfamilies are so pervasively represented in terms of disruption, upheaval and emotional turmoil. However closely stepfamilies may resemble the conventional nuclear family, ultimately they are perceived as second-best in terms of 'children's needs'. Nevertheless, it is generally recognised that re-partnering can provide a route out of poverty for many lone mothers. Merging motherhood with a heterosexual partnership to form a new 'family' was a positive experience for several of the mothers in the sample, conferring greater moral, financial and practical capital as well as offering them a potentially fulfilling adult relationship. Although as Sally's experience demonstrates, investing in a new partnership can be a highly risky strategy leading to greater financial and personal vulnerably.

Becoming a stepfamily – Sally's story

Sally explained how she met and married her first husband Frank while she was still in her teens. Having experienced an unhappy and violent childhood, she left home to live in a bedsit and met Frank shortly afterwards. At the time he had four children of his own living with him, and so Sally moved in both as his wife and as a stepmother to his children. Reflecting back, Sally described how the children significantly contributed to the attraction she felt towards Frank. She had desperately wanted to work with children on leaving school and emphasised her frustration at having to give up her first job in a children's home because the pay was not enough to cover board money for her parents:

I just went in very naive. I mean, I was 19 years old. And here I was landed with these four children and that was it. In the end what was I in there for? The relationship with Frank or the kids?

And the two came hand in hand.

Yeah.

And when you moved in you took on the role of a mother really?

Yeah, nobody else had that role. And of course all the children were craving for that attention, you know a female. . . . I know it sounds really strange, but I don't think I ever really thought about it. I just did it and that was that. . . . It's very hard to look back and think what I was thinking then. Because I'm so different now to what I was then.

> Then I suppose I would have been quite happy with the way things were, and almost if you like grateful that I was able to do it. It's just the way things are so different . . . It's hard to look back on something and think of the way you were when you were 19.

Marrying Frank had seemed like an opportunity to continue caring for children while building her own family, but shortly after their marriage Frank began drinking heavily and behaving aggressively. Sally stayed with him for eight years and had three children of her own (Ricky, Mel and Andy), but he became increasingly violent and abusive towards her. Although she regularly considered leaving him, she felt powerless to act with seven children depending on her. Worrying that she would be unable to cope with any more children in the context of Frank's violence, she had a sterilisation operation shortly after the birth of Andy.

Frank's violence worsened and finally became unbearable. Anxious both about her own safety and the effects on the children, Sally eventually packed her bags, collected her own three children and went to the local social services office. They referred her on to what she termed a 'halfway house', a cross between a bed-and-breakfast and a hostel. At the time, Sally's step-children were in their teenage years and she had felt they were more capable of looking after themselves. However, shortly after Sally left Frank, his 15-year-old daughter Jane walked into a police station, asked for Sally to be sent for, and reported that she had been sexually abused by her father:

> When she was being interviewed she had to have an adult there, and she asked for me to be there. And it was harrowing. I mean, it's horrible to have to hear, but in a way it was good that I did because there could have been no doubt that she was telling the truth. Simply because she made an 11, 12-page statement and you can't make up that amount of information. I mean, she wasn't sure about dates and things like that, but she could remember things by what had happened that day or things that had happened later in the evening.

The children living with Frank were immediately taken into care and court proceedings were initiated. During this time, Frank moved out of the house and Sally was able to move back in again with her three children. She explained how, despite the overwhelming evidence, Frank's case never made it to court:

Things were different then. He never got charged. He was arrested but they said that they couldn't take it to court because she was so damaged psychologically she wouldn't be able to stand up in the witness box.

Oh, that's terrible.

Yeah. She was damaged internally. She had to have an operation. But things were different then, weren't they.

Although Frank was not supposed to have contact with any of his children, he started coming to Sally's house shortly after the case had been dropped. Sally's brother eventually intervened and frightened him off with threats of physical violence, but Sally still felt unable to settle in the house:

Where you worried that he was going to come after you?

Oh, he did. A few times. He broke in. When I came back from school he was there. In the end I moved, because I felt that while I stayed here he saw it as his home. So I had to move.

Sally organised a transfer with the council to a different part of the borough. She found herself having to deal with the upheaval of moving and the challenge of managing on state benefits. She also described how during this time she was plagued with social workers who behaved as though she was to blame for what had happened to Jane. Case conferences were arranged to discuss the future of her children and to Sally's horror, Frank was eventually granted supervised contact with them once a month. When Frank later met and moved in with another woman, social workers stopped supervising the contact and the children were expected to visit him on the first Saturday of every month. Sally explained how Andy invariably refused to go, and how on reaching 11 or 12 Ricky and Mel both stopped the contact of their own accord. According to Sally, Frank made no real effort to stay in touch with them.

Sally met Martin soon after she had moved and filed for a divorce from Frank. She got talking to him at a friend's birthday celebration at a pub, and began seeing him regularly. Martin moved in with Sally and the children a few months later and they planned to get married once the divorce came through. Sally emphasised how well the children got on with him, and how they began calling him 'Dad'. Six months after Martin moved in, Sally was stunned to find she was pregnant, in spite of her previous sterilisation operation. While Joel was welcomed as a happy accident, the births of Jamie, Brad and Jack were intended and planned for. Sally explained how, for a while, they had an extremely happy family life. They got married shortly after Joel was born, and according to Sally, Martin actively involved himself in changing nappies and caring for all of the children. However, a few years after their marriage, Sue described how Martin began going out regularly, often staying out all night. Sally suspected he was seeing other women, and eventually had her fears were confirmed when he left while she was still pregnant with Jack, to live with someone else.

Sally was forced to claim welfare benefits and stressed how difficult it was making ends meet with seven children to care for. She described how she managed to feed and clothe the children, with the help of regular food parcels from the church and loans from social services, but explained how there was never any money left for any extras such as toys or sweets:

> You don't live on it [welfare benefit], you exist. It's enough to stop you starving but it's not enough for your children to have anything. I don't expect luxuries, but even pensioners get £10 at Christmas. There I was with nothing. Well, I used to get the food parcels from social services. I did. And blooming grateful I was for them as well.

Martin contributed little financially, but carried on seeing his sons regularly for the first year after he left. From then on his contact with them became less routine, and eventually tailed off to just birthdays, Christmas and Easter.

It was while her younger children were staying with their father that Sally met Ian in a local pub. She began seeing him regularly, but explained how she made a conscious decision not to introduce him to the children. She kept the relationship casual at first, explaining that she was not 'looking for another dad for the kids'. She also described how she found out a few months into the relationship that Ian was married with a young baby (Shelly). Although Sally had initially been shocked at this discovery, she continued seeing Ian. After a few years, his wife returned to full-time work and a baby sitter was needed for Shelly. Ian was working nights as a security guard, so he would bring Shelly to Sally's house in the morning and stay until the afternoon. With Ian spending so much time at Sally's house, he got to know the other children well, and developed a close relationship with the younger boys.

Eventually, Ian's relationship with his wife ended when she met and moved in with someone else, leaving him to care for Shelly. Ian and Shelly then officially moved in with Sally and the other children. Sally described this as a particularly difficult year, emphasising the overcrowding in the house and the jealousy which emerged between Shelly and Sally's youngest boys. After a while the strain became too much, and following a traumatic experience of losing her sister to cancer, she decided she could not continue living with Ian in such difficult circumstances. After a big row Ian went back to live with his mother, while Shelly went to live with her mother. For Sally this temporary separation allowed her some much needed time and space, heading off a complete breakdown. After a month or so, Sally felt able to start seeing Ian again and he moved back in shortly after. A compromise was reached concerning Shelly, and she remained with her mother during the week and stayed with Sally, Ian and the other children at weekends.

This new arrangement eased the pressure in the family, until a fire broke out in the house. No one was hurt, but several rooms in the house were made uninhabitable. Initially the younger boys stayed with their father, but once it became clear the council would not re-house them immediately, they returned to live with Sally, Ian and two of the older children (Mel and Andy), in a house consisting of just three usable rooms and a charred kitchen and bathroom. All five of the boys slept in the largest bedroom, Mel slept in the smaller bedroom, sharing it with Shelly at weekends, while Sally and Ian slept down in the lounge. This cramped and stressful arrangement was alleviated slightly when Mel left to live with her boyfriend, but the overcrowding continued for months until a new four-bedroom house was found for them by the council.

Prominent in Sally's account was a sense of powerlessness resulting from her low economic status. Financial struggle was experienced as an inevitable feature of her life, forcing her into situations and actions against her will. Lack of money sabotaged her aspirations to work with children on leaving school and helped bind her to a violent abusive relationship for eight years. While she was eventually able to leave Frank, this action was not articulated as a choice, and was characterised by destitution, uncertainty and danger. Being left by her second husband to care and provide for seven children further highlighted her precarious financial position, as did the serious house fire. She views her current situation with Gary as far from ideal:

It's not how I would have liked it to be. And I think Shelly living with us for that year knocked our relationship so much, and also the children's. And Ian has her every weekend now, I say Ian but we have her every weekend. And in a way, I know it sounds unfair, but it's that same strain again. It's just so hard. I mean, me and him work hard all week to have a stress-free weekend but we never do. . . . I believe in marriage. I really, really, really do believe in marriage, but I wouldn't marry him because I know it would end in divorce.

Why's that?

I just don't think that we're a perfect couple, if you like. Not perfect, there's no such thing as a perfect couple. I just don't see years and years ahead me and him being together . . . We argue too much . . . We start arguing about very small minor things. It just escalates. It starts off silly and it ends up his family and everything. . . . I don't think we ever resolve things. We just have like a cooling off period. I think there's just so much resentment around me and my children towards his family and from them.

Nevertheless, Sally acknowledges the practical and financial advantages gained from having a partner. With Ian working full-time night shifts he was able to pay for her vocational course in nursery care at college, and when necessary look after the children during the day. Sally now works full-time in a nursery. Though their dual income is modest it considerably eases the financial strain of providing for such a large family.

Sally's hesitancy about the future is not surprising given her previous experiences of relationship breakdown. Accounts given by other mothers in the sample similarly highlight the potential risks and benefits of trading lone motherhood for the greater economic security of a heterosexual partnership. Like Sally, Kelly (discussed in Chapter 5) had to flee a seriously abusive relationship with the father of her children and was forced to relocate several times to different parts of the country before meeting her current partner, Terry. She remembers only too well the deprivation and hardship associated with raising children alone on benefits:

Money was very, very hard then. We was on the social then and we was paying the bills and that, and there was days where I just didn't eat or if I went shopping I'd just buy a packet of fishfingers and a loaf of bread and that would do me all week and that. But the kids, I always made sure that they had what they needed, and I'd actually go and borrow if I needed to for the kids. But I'd go without, sometime I had nothing to eat, not anything, just drink water and that would be my day. But the kids never went without because I used to sort of turn up at someone's house at meal times and that so the kids got fed.

Kelly now cares for Terry's 6-year-old daughter from a previous relationship as well as her own two children while he works full time as a lorry driver. However, while the family now have a steady income and a comfortable rented house, Kelly's 9-year-old son is exhibiting severe behavioural difficulties stemming from the abuse and insecurity of their previous life. His behaviour is placing Kelly and Terry's relationship under strain, highlighting the precariousness of her current financial security. If they were to break up, Kelly would risk loosing her home and would again be reliant on state benefits.

Employed but poor: socially included families?

The notion that paid employment is the only morally acceptable route out of poverty pervades current government thinking in the UK, and can impact harshly on working-class mothers and their children. As I have outlined, many mothers need financial and practical help to extricate themselves and their children from violence and abuse. The poverty and stigma attached to becoming a lone mother on benefits ensure that escaping from a damaging relationship is often pursued as last resort and is characterised by risk, trauma and deprivation. The communitarian focus on citizenship and the virtues of paid employment promote an expectation that any reliance on state benefits should be temporary. Yet this approach fails to engage with the impoverishment, injustice and marginalisation faced by parents forced to depend on low-paid, insecure and often arduous jobs, as the example of Meena and her husband demonstrate.

Working for the children – Meena's story

Meena grew up in a Sikh family in a semi-rural part of India and trained to be a teacher before marrying her husband Sal. At the time Sal was living and working in London as a leather manufacturer. They married in India but Sal returned to England after the wedding while Meena stayed behind. Their intention was to move to London and raise a family but Sal's work dried up as a result of an economic recession, and they feared his insecure employment would jeopardise Meena's application for residency in the UK. Sal spent as much time in India as he could and Meena soon fell pregnant with their first son, Raj (now 11). Their second son Apu (now 9) was also born in India. Eventually Sal landed a steady job manufacturing leather goods for large department stores. Meena was granted residency and travelled with the two boys to settle with Sal in a rented flat in London. Meena remembers this as a particularly demanding and depressing time. Sal worked very long hours and would often bring bits of leather work home which she would help out with. She missed her family deeply and felt very isolated. She had received lots of help with the children in India and having to care for them all by herself was a tough adjustment to make:

> The most difficult thing is that to look after the children by own, alone. My husband used to work [far away] London side so he used to go 6 o'clock and he used to come back 10 o'clock in the evening. I had to do all the things. To take them playgroup; they used to go to play-group when they were small, so take them my own, come back and then again go and pick them up. Cooking and shopping . . . it was very difficult with the children and at that time I haven't got any car. . . . So that one year was very suffering for me . . . with the raining and snowing and I have to take the kids on my own.

Despite his hard work, Sal's factory was forced to close and he lost his job. Although a skilled tradesman, Sal realised there was little future in manufacturing in the UK and he signed up to work for a large contract cleaning service. In the meantime the family were allocated a small two-bedroom council flat on a low-rise estate, which they accepted gratefully. Sal works 5 days a week in shifts, from 5 o'clock till midnight for one company and then works for another firm until 3 p.m. He earns the minimum wage, has no job security and limited sick pay. A number of years after moving to the UK Meena had a third son, Rega (now 2½). When the family became eligible to buy their council flat Meena also began working in an attempt to save for a deposit. Although she originally trained as a teacher in India Meena did not want to pursue this option in England. Her English is functional but basic, and gaining the appropriate qualifications would be a struggle. During the day Meena works part-time as a contract cleaner 7 days a week, and then goes off to sell cosmetic products door to door when her shift finishes. Both Meena and Sal deliver leaflets at weekends. In an attempt to move into better paid and more secure employment, Meena has also begun voluntary work with a friend whose job involves providing support and advice to the local Sikh community. She is hoping this might lead to a permanent post in the future.

While Meena is at work and the older boys are at school, Sal looks after little Rega. This means he has very few hours sleep before he has to care for an energetic, boisterous 2½-year-old. Meena has made an arrangement with a neighbour who often comes round for a couple of hours a day while Sal sleeps. The same neighbour also helps out by taking Rega while Meena picks the older boys up from school. This gruelling schedule leaves both parents exhausted, but they are driven by their determination to make a better life for their children. Purchasing their council flat is viewed as a vital future investment for the boys, but money is also spent on toys, computer equipment and games and brand-name clothing. As Meena makes clear, the children's needs and wants are prioritised:

> When we have a child our own life goes other side. We have to do all things according to our children's future. Because at present the kids are small it means that they can't do anything on their own, so we are doing for them only, so we won't see our side much, only the children things. Doing everything for kids only.

As I will outline in more detail in Chapter 6, providing specific material goods for children can have a great emotional significance for working-class families, but in this case there was also a practical aim. Their council estate was becoming increasingly dangerous for the two older boys, who often found themselves under attack from racially segregated gangs of teenagers. Meena and Sal were distraught and determined to keep their sons away from trouble. They provided a playstation, computer and television in the boys bedroom in an attempt to entice the children to stay indoors and out of harm's way.

While the family remain above the official poverty threshold, their income is very low and their jobs are vulnerable and could disappear overnight. Social critics like Barbara Ehrenreich and Polly Tonybee have highlighted the hidden strains and burdens carried by the 'working poor' in low-wage, insecure jobs. Barbara Ehrenreich's (2001) stint as an undercover journalist in the US 'unskilled' labour market revealed the extent of skills and determination required to sustain the repetitive and mundane tasks associated with these jobs. She emphasised the stamina, speed, dexterity and quick-thinking displayed by her fellow workers, and described how she found herself unable to deal with the work-related stress and overload she faced. Polly Toynbee (2003) details a similar experience in the UK context. For Meena and Sal, earning enough means working unfeasibly long hours and surviving on little sleep. Nevertheless, Meena is strikingly resourceful and determined to pursue any opportunities that present themselves. She helps out regularly at her local temple and ensures that the family benefits from the classes, food and childcare opportunities this involvement generates. She also makes sure she signs up for any free short courses that are running in the community:

> Because I like to be doing some courses, I do lots of courses to gain knowledge. I attend one youth club. It was a one-day course, I have a certificate of that. I start basic course, skill course, you know skill course different courses, first aid and things like that. So I did that even. Once I joined a beauty course.
>
> A beauty course as well, are you still doing that?
>
> Yes. Because my hobby, I cut my own kids hair, I do cut from 6, 7 years. So I joined one basic course even for cutting hair, styling and all. I like to join small small courses which is handy and things to get you through life just run smoothly and nicely. It's easy for me to cut hair, because at home you cut anytime even Saturday, Sunday any day or night, you don't have to go to take them to barber shop.
>
> It's very handy.
>
> It's very handy, it's one way of saving money.

Since moving into their council flat Meena and Sal have been driven by a desire to own the property rather than rent it. While very homely and cosy with pictures of family lining the walls, the flat is claustrophobically small. The two older boys share a box room with bunk beds, while Meena, Sal and Rega sleep in a slightly larger back bedroom. The estate is bleak, in a state of disrepair and located beside a large, busy dual carriage way that has to be crossed to reach shops or transport. The area is also blighted by drugs and violent crime. Yet Meena and Sal are resolute in their determination to save enough money to take advantage of a subsidy offered to council tenents able to purchase their properties. They are aware in the context of spiralling house prices in London that this is the only chance they will have to buy their own home. Both are emotionally as well as financially invested in the notion of having something concrete to pass on to their sons. However, this is dependent on the couple scraping together enough deposit money to secure a mortgage. Saving towards this has been a painfully slow process and is complicated by their obligation to send money back to relatives in India from time to time.

Over a period of 8 years Meena and Sal had been able to save £3,500 but were still a long way off what they needed. Speculation that the government subsidy to encourage council tenants to buy their properties might be scrapped added to the stress. When Meena's friends and neighbours began discussing a financial opportunity that seemed too good to be true, the couple's desperation lured them to make a large investment. The scheme was an infamous pyramid scam called 'Women Empowering Women' and was presented to Meena as a way for women in the community to support each other. To join she was required to make a hefty donation to the group leader, the elderly neighbour of a much-trusted friend. Meena was assured that in time large sums of money would soon flow back to her as other members joined and paid subscriptions. The pyramid fell apart before Meena saw a penny, leaving her and Sal shocked and hurt. Feelings of betrayal were particularly hard for Meena to come to terms with, as she had been led to believe the scheme would be of mutual benefit to all the women involved:

I don't mind to work hard, but I can't steal somebody's money. I don't want to snatch anybody's money because I believe, we can work hard, we are working you know. My husband and me we are working hard, but we don't want to be rich on somebody else money.

So how did you know her in the first place?

Because just passing by and she's my friend, Suba, and that old lady she is living upstairs of her.

She lives upstairs from your friend?

Yes. So when I go to my friend she is sometimes downstairs and we say hello, because she is old lady we say 'Hello Auntie', this we do and that's it. She know me 8, 9 years from this place, she know me very well. She know what kind of people we are.

Although the couple went to the police, they were told no action could be taken because Meena had paid the old lady in cash. They have now come to terms with loosing the money but they have not given up on the dream of buying their flat. Sal is close to raising the necessary deposit in loans from friends, relatives and acquaintances, although the repayment terms are far from clear. As such the family's future is filled with risk and uncertainty. They are gambling on being able to repay a mortgage and several loans on poorly-paid, insecure jobs. They cannot afford any periods of illness, something their overburdened schedules must make them more prone to. If they do slide into debt they will likely be at the mercy of moneylenders and may lose their flat altogether. While the couple's resolve and resilience cannot be underestimated, their situation is precarious and raises numerous questions about social justice in relation to low-wage employment.

Conclusion: managing vulnerability

Deprivation and economic hardship have led to a range of different circumstances for the mothers in the sample, but the more fundamental meaning of managing with very little money or resources is similar across accounts. All the mothers are engaged in a day-to-day struggle to survive and ensure that their children are provided for. Each has experienced powerlessness and lack of control as a result of economic dependence and all are well aware of the extent to which their actions are restricted and constrained. Still, as the brief case studies in this chapter demonstrate, the mothers coped with limited access to economic and material capital while striving for better lives, often taking risks in the hope of improving conditions for themselves and their children. In the face of danger, insecurity and destitution they coped by building a 'ledge' from which they could arrest further free-fall and plan a forward trajectory. Some gambled with benefit fraud, others placed a stake in a new partner, while others took on debt. These risks are calculated to bring benefits, but the mothers and their children face drastic consequences if they misfire. Sam could face prison if her cash-in-hand work is discovered. Sally might have to return to the poverty of welfare benefits if Ian leaves her to care for the children, and Meena could loose her savings and her home. Advantages gained are invariably offset by increased insecurity and vulnerability. When things go wrong it is easy for these women's actions to be portrayed as foolish or irresponsible. They live a catch-22 situation in which they are routinely denigrated for their failure to change and improve while being castigated when their inevitably risky but proactive strategies fall short.

In this chapter I have tried to highlight the significance of the material and physical in mothers' accounts of their lives. Using case studies and particular examples I have sought to show how lack of money, limited practical support and restricted power shape the women's lives on a basic level, constraining and compelling choices. But these effects can also be traced more systematically at a specific level, revealing their effect on subjectivity, values and practices. In the remaining chapters of this book I will explore how the materiality of class delimits and predisposes understandings and actions.

Examining the grounded nature of meaning and experience draws attention to the formative nature of particular factors. This is explored in more detail in the next chapter where the focus shifts to working-class mothers' understandings of personhood.

Chapter 4

Class, subjectivity and motherhood

Structural and social relations have a major impact on the perception of self and others. In Chapter 2, I outlined how the middle classes came to construct themselves as distinct from a working-class mass, and argued that individuality remains a marker of moral superiority. In this chapter I will explore alternative working-class subjectivities and demonstrate how they can represent a challenge to middle-class individualist values. More specifically I draw on working-class mothers' accounts of their lives and their children to reveal a more relational experience of self. Moving from a general discussion of personhood and disadvantage I focus on the particular accounts given by Liz and Sally to highlight class-specific meanings and values around child development. The real lived consequences of a contemporary backward slide towards individualised understandings of class are also laid out in this chapter. I show how working-class families are used as markers of individual failure, enabling the middle classes to distinguish themselves as rational, autonomous, reflexive selves and thereby claim an apparently natural entitlement to privilege.

Relational selves

In her longitudinal ethnographic study, Beverly Skeggs (1997) highlights the failure of contemporary theories of the self to engage with the different way in which working-class women 'do subjectivity'. Most theoretical accounts of the subject are structured by an assumption of individualism that originates from and benefits the privileged middle classes. The ideal of the individual can work to justify those with power and authority while branding other groups as inferior for their lack of differentiation. Selective distribution of the cultural resources underpinning agentic, reflexive selves conveys entitlement and recognition of moral worth. The women in Skeggs' study had restricted access to a discourse of individualism and did not assume that they had individual rights or a status that was valuable or even interesting. As a result they had less investment in their own subjectivity and their reflexivity was more connected to others.

Being an individual self in Western society is to some extent compulsory, but being the 'right' kind of self is dependent on one's social and structural position. The working-class mothers featured in this book narrated their own and their children's lives by drawing on dominant constructions of individuality and personal development, yet they are simultaneously positioned within these discourses as lacking. There is little space to recognise and explore alternative understandings of self and other that underpin lives and experiences. Feminist writers such as Carol Gilligan (1982) and Seyla Benhabib (1986) have long critiqued the concept of the 'autonomous ego' that has underpinned Western approaches to social theory, questioning the premise of the individuated, disembodied subject. Instead they have formulated conceptions of autonomy that emphasise mutuality, relatedness and recognition of the needs of the other.

Selma Sevenhuijsen (2002) suggests that this relational ontology is encapsulated in a feminist 'ethic of care' which offers an alternative to the particular interpretations of subjectivity, morality and justice that charaterise the work of Ulrick and Elizabeth Beck, Antony Giddens and other contemporary social theorists. Viewed from this alternative standpoint individuals exist because of and through their relationships with others, and cannot be regarded as separate, individualised subjects. Rather than exploring how separate individuals negotiate and maintain connections with others, feminists taking an ethic of care approach assume inter-dependency and examine how personal freedom is articulated within a framework of obligation and relational morality. This approach is based on a recognition of gender difference, but as I show in this chapter class is equally significant in shaping how selves and others might be conceptualised.

Highly individualised developmental models of childrearing tend to resonate with white, middle-class parents, while pathologising alternative understandings and practices of working-class and ethnic minority mothers (Ribbens McCarthy and Edwards 2002). Disadvantaged parents are commonly portrayed as too selfish to care for others. Yet across the years the relational and intimate nature of working-class culture has consistently emerged as research findings. A number of classic community studies conducted in the 1950s and 1960s challenged negative stereotypes of the urban poor by revealing the crucial significance of working-class solidarity in the day-to-day lives of families. These studies demonstrated the key role that mothers in particular played in mediating and maintaining three-generational family structures characterised by a system of mutual aid and support (Firth 1956; Young and Wilmot 1957; Townsend 1957; Rosser and Harris 1965; Firth *et al.* 1969). Despite dominant narratives about the decline of social cohesion and trust, contemporary research continues to highlight the embedded nature of working-class life (Skeggs 1997; Mitchell and Green 2002; Lareau 2003; MacDonald *et al.* 2005).

This more relational experience of self can be illustrated by drawing more specifically on data from the *Resources in Parenting* project. Our focus on parents' social networks revealed class-differentiated configurations of support and conditionality characterising the social connections of families. The highly gendered nature of these social interactions ran across class, in that it was predominantly mothers who maintained and managed social relationships. However, the quality and meaning of these relationships differed in line with class location. In general, working-class parents were more likely to describe a core network of highly reciprocal, supportive relationships supplemented by connections to more peripheral social contacts. Middle-class parents, in comparison, discussed their attachment to a more dispersed and less bonded social group, with few obligations or responsibilities beyond socialising (see Gillies and Edwards 2006 for more details).

For these working-class mothers close social relationships carry enormous significance. Many rely on, and are relied upon, by family members and friends for emotional, practical and financial support. This kind of inter-dependency is experienced and articulated in terms of crucial and much valued attachments. Longstanding and much trusted friends are often defined as family, with the word symbolising mutual commitment and loyalty. For example, Denise's relationship with her best friend, Josie, illustrates the intensity of the bond they have established:

Josie, she'll do anything I ask her to. If she can help me she will. She has a car. If I want to go somewhere she'll take me. But only last week Liam had a sick day off of school and I needed to go shopping and she came from school and sat with him. I only rang her at quarter past 8 and she were here at twenty to 9 and I'd do the same thing for her. Um, we do help each other out, and she won't take for things . . . You know like if she's out and about, like you said before, she'll ring me from wherever she is and say 'I've seen such a thing, it's so much, do you want me to get ya?' And I do the same with her . . . I mean the day me mum died she rang me at 11, me mum died at ten past 11 and Josie rung me at about 12 minutes past 11, didn't she, and she said 'Denise', she said 'I'm in the middle of me washing', she said 'but I've got a funny feeling something's happened'. And I told her what had happened, and within ten minutes – I mean Josh then, her lad, he were only baby and she were down here and she just never went home. And she knew, that's how close we are, she knew something had happened.

Bagnell, Longhurst and Savage (2003) identified a similar class-based distinction in their study of networks and social capital, with parents from working-class areas demonstrating tighter social ties, while parents from middle-class areas described more diffuse networks. As they showed, the working-class residents tended to be more tightly embedded in local communities than their more mobile and less restricted middle-class counterparts. Our research also revealed the way social relationships are grounded in particular material circumstances and lived accordingly. Take the contrasting examples of Julie, an African-Caribbean lone mother on welfare benefits, and Katherine, a white middle-class lone mother from the wider *Resources in Parenting* sample.

Julie has two children by different fathers. Her youngest daughter, Carly, is 10 and her older son, Lloyd, is 15. She rents a housing association property on a purpose-built estate in a crowded urban area populated by high numbers of long-term unemployed, students and lone mothers. Julie describes her relationship with family members as very close. She has a particularly strong interdependent relationship with one of her sisters. They have children of similar ages and Julie provides childcare for her sister to allow her to work. In turn Julie receives strong emotional and practical support from her sister and financial help, for example, in the form of grocery shopping. Julie also emphasises the close contact she maintains with the rest of her family, by regularly speaking on the phone and visiting. She views these family relationships as a support safety net and has received (and provided) practical help in the past. Julie has a large network of friends that she regularly socialises with, although she distinguishes them from her 'genuine' friends who she feels have become part of her family. She has two particularly good ('genuine') friends living nearby with children of their own who she relies on for emotional and practical support. She is also godmother to another friend's daughter and a neighbour's daughter and provides regular childcare for them.

Katherine has two daughters, Zoe, age 9, and Adele, age 5, and has recently separated from her husband. They live in large detached house in a small village in the home counties. She works three days a week as a lawyer and her annual household income (including contributions from her husband) exceeds £100,000. Her neighbours are mainly other highly educated professionals and business owners. Katherine has lived the area for the past seven years and has no family members living nearby. She does not have a close relationship with her parents and has rarely asked them for help or support. Katherine's husband (a full-time lawyer) takes the children at weekends. Katherine has a good relationship with her neighbours and feels that she lives in a 'great community'. Most of Katherine's neighbours have children of their own and they socialise regularly. Although Katherine's employs a childminder three days a week, her children spend a lot of time next door playing with the neighbours' children. Katherine describes a close relationship with the female neighbours either side of her and feels they were particularly supportive when she was splitting up with her husband. She regularly holidays with her neighbours and a friend from work. Katherine is also involved with the school's Parent Teachers Association (PTA) and as a result has built relationships with her daughters' teachers and other local parents.

Julie and Katherine are clearly both well networked, but the social relationships they rely on and access on a daily basis are rooted in their very different social and economic circumstances. Julie struggles to make ends meet on welfare benefits, while Katherine's financial independence enables her to combine social relationships with paid-for services to secure any help she needs. As well as employing a childminder three days and one evening a week, Katherine also pays for the children to attend regular after-school activities such as French, chess and swimming. Although she has less need of informal support, she benefits on a personal and emotional level from maintaining reciprocal relationships with neighbours, friends and other mothers. More significantly, differences are apparent in terms of the value and meaning of the social resources each mother provides and acquires through their networks. Julie has time and experience of raising children and is able to provide invaluable childcare help to her sister and other friends. In return, Julie's shopping is often collected and bought for her, while the goodwill she generates stands as a potential future resource if practical or financial help is needed. As a result Julie's social relationships translate into the practical help and psychological support that enable day-to-day survival. For Julie, this is experienced in terms of strong emotional bonds with particular individuals, and is expressed as a form of familial interdependency. Like many of the working-class mothers in this book, she makes a clear distinction between acquaintances and family, and includes close friends in the later category:

> Like the circle of, like, people I move with, or me family I should say – not so much people because, like I said I'm not one for like having lots and lots of friends, I've acquaintances – because like we help each other, you know, we support each other.

In contrast, Katherine's high social status and privilege have enabled her to build relationships with other wealthy and relatively powerful individuals, which (alongside the pleasure of friendship) can be drawn on in a selective and often highly instrumental way. For example, she describes how she joined the local PTA in order to network locally for the benefit of herself and the children. This more instrumental focus on the personal benefits of social networking was implicit in many of the interviews with middle-class parents in the Resources in Parenting project. Such individualistic values were distinctly at odds with the obligation, commitment and dependency characterising the denser networks of friends and family associated with working-class families (Gillies and Edwards 2006). These stronger personal investments in friends and family members involved hard work and dedication. These mothers cared for friends and family when they were ill, provided regular unpaid childcare, looked after elderly neighbours and relatives and lent small 'tide-over' amounts of money. While most had bene-fited in kind through these types of supportive networks, they are maintained through a de-centring of self-interest.

Nevertheless, it is important not to romanticise such tight-knit relation-ships. While they are the source of great pleasure and allow mothers to 'get by' on a basic level, they place heavy demands on time and energy. Narratives of betrayal, disloyalty and estrangement are common, reflecting the high expectations and emotional intensity associated with them (Gillies and Edwards 2006). Significantly, though, these kinds of social bonds are sustained through a lack of prioritisation of self that is at odds with dominant individualistic values. In failing to embrace the logic of self-interest struc-turing capitalist ideology, these mothers come to be seen as a threat to its reproduction.

As I outlined in Chapter 1, the current policy preoccupation with parenting is strongly tied to particular understandings of development and subjectivity. It is reasoned that meritocracy will follow if working-class parents can be taught to raise their children as middle-class selves. Aside from the faulty logic of using class-specific parenting practices to account for the inequality they reflect, this notion imposes a value-laden interpretation of self. As Steph Lawler (2000) notes, it is through the nurturing of individuality that children become recognised as social beings and 'good citizens'. Working-class subjectivity is condemned as lacking the reflexivity and determination to enable personal improvement, as well as the knowledge and skills to raise their children to be the right kind of selves (Gillies 2005b).

Individualism and the cultivated child

In her detailed ethnographic study of class, race and American family life, Annette Lareau (2003) notes how approaches to childrearing are deeply classed in terms of values and practices. She shows how middle-class parents engage in a process of 'concerted cultivation', in order to develop particular skills and traits in their children. This often involves a tight timetable of organised activities managed and overseen by parents, leaving children with little time to themselves. Lareau demonstrates how daily middle-class family life is commonly structured around a range of after-school activities which shape the self. This 'cultivational' approach to childrearing facilitates the construction of the proficient middle-class individual able to exploit the opportunities that frame their lives:

> By encouraging involvement in activities outside of the home, middle-class parents position their children to receive more than an education in how to play soccer, baseball or piano. These young sports enthusiasts and budding musicians acquire skills and dispositions that help them navigate the institutional world. They learn to think of themselves as special and as entitled to receive certain kinds of services from adults. They also acquire a valuable set of white collar work skills, including how to set priorities, manage an itinerary, shake hands with strangers and work on a team.
>
> (Lareau 2003: 39)

Lareau also observed how interactions between middle-class parents and their children are similarly orientated towards the development of personal skills, with an emphasis on reasoning and negotiation. This approach has parallels with the discourse of 'sensitive mothering' identified and deconstructed in Valerie Walkerdine and Helen Lucey's (1989) classic study *Democracy in the Kitchen*. Walkerdine and Lucey demonstrated how middle-class childrearing practices are articulated as normal and desirable through the language of developmental psychology. As such they are accepted as self-evident markers of 'good parenting', particularly in comparison with representations of ignorant and insensitive working-class practices. The material and structural underpinnings of parenting are concealed behind a projected façade of preference and (ir)rationality.

As I argued in Chapter 2, a contemporary fixation on individualisation and democratisation have prompted a new concern that subjects adapt to the changing post-industrial landscape described by prominent sociological theorists. The UK government's preoccupation with childhood development, and more specifically in the nurturing of young selves by their parents, represents an effort to mould individual subjectivity in order to produce the 'responsible risk-takers' of the future. There is strikingly little recognition that the individualised, agentic self theorised by the Becks and Giddens and valorised in UK government policies requires access to middle-class economic, cultural, social and emotional capital. As I will demonstrate, working-class parents and their children are not just out of reach of this model of the worthy subject, they are actively positioned as 'other' to affirm the individuality and superiority of their middle-class counterparts.

Standing out and fitting in

The *Resources in Parenting* study revealed the extent to which the middle-class interviewees were invested in constructing their children as 'unique' and distinct from others (Gillies 2005b). Education was the principle way of conceptualising 'specialness', with middle-class parents commonly emphasising the intellectual sophistication of their offspring. While almost all of the middle-class parents in the sample used the term 'bright' to describe their children, this word was strikingly absent from most working-class vocabularies. As Helen Lucey and Diane Reay (2002) demonstrate, the notion that middle-class children are bright, clever and possess potential is a common implicit assumption articulated by their parents, teachers and the children themselves. In their school-based research they show how middle-class children were most likely to be identified as 'gifted and talented', thereby qualifying for educational acceleration and enhancement schemes designed for bright but socially disadvantaged inner-city children.

But 'brightness' is not a stand-alone concept. It is necessarily constructed in relation to the alternatives of being average or 'dim'. Operating as part of a discourse of entitlement, the notion of the 'bright' child stakes a moral claim of exceptionality. Middle-class parents commonly use the term to stress their child's right to attention and academic success. However, in order for their children to be exceptional and deserving of the investments made in their development, other (working-class) children must exist as markers of failure or ordinariness. This process of distinction lies at the heart of the education system (Bourdieu and Passeron 1977) and exposes a major flaw in efforts to associate social inequality with parenting skills. Middle-class selves are necessarily defined in relation to working-class inferiority, with claims to privilege founded on a notion of deserving individuality. But as I have outlined, such middle-class selves are grounded in a social and economic context which enables, supports and warrants their individuality. In the absence of a structural framework conveying autonomy and legitimisation, standing out from the crowd is likely to be experienced in terms of vulnerability and notoriety (Gillies 2005b).

Beverly Skeggs (1997) argues that the ontological security of the working classes is more likely to lie in 'fitting in' rather than standing out. This certainly accords with the different values held by the working-class mothers featured in this book. As well as articulating a more relational sense of self, the mothers were often at pains to present their sons and daughters as being 'no worse' and 'as good as' other children. Rather than emphasising the significance of exceptional 'brightness', working-class mothers proudly highlighted their children's ability to stay out of trouble, get on with others, and work hard. These mothers were distinctly more likely to attach negative connotations to the notion of children being different or 'special', fearing that any marking out would be associated with accusations of misbehaviour or failure. This concern is further underlined by Diane Reay and Helen Lucey's (2000) research into secondary school transition, highlighting working-class children's desire to avoid standing out as different in school. Discomfort with the principles of individualism is effectively demonstrated through a detailed focus on Liz, a white, re-partnered mother with three sons. The example of Liz illustrates how understandings of childhood development are culturally grounded, leading to class-specific parenting practices. As I will show, the individualistic principles underpinning democratic parenting values may be viewed as risky and irresponsible by those lacking middle-class legitimacy.

Liz – children need to 'knuckle down'

Liz lives with her partner, Eddie, and her three sons in a small ex-council house in a working-class suburb. Eddie is the father of her youngest son (4-year-old Calum). Her two elder sons (Scott aged 10 and Adam aged 13) are from her previous marriage to Pete. Liz had married Pete when she was 19 and had Adam four years later, having worked as a waitress since she left school. She found motherhood difficult and isolating at first. Although she grew more confident with the years, she became increasingly frustrated and disillusioned with her marriage. At the time their lives revolved around trying to save money for a mortgage. Pete was morose, withdrawn and appeared to have little interest in the boys. When Scott was two and Adam was five she went back to work part-time in a newly opened pub close to where she lived. Pete (a delivery driver) agreed to look after the children three evenings a week while Liz did bar work. Although the money she earned was poor, she enjoyed chatting to the regulars and the other staff members and looked forward to her work nights.

Liz's resentment towards Pete came to a head when she met Eddie, and she decided she should end her marriage. After a long and acrimonious divorce and bitterly fought custody battle, an arrangement was made whereby the boys would spend every weekend with their father. This freed up time for Liz to spend with Eddie, and not long after she fell pregnant with Calum. Although the boys were happy and excited about the new baby, introducing her sons to Eddie was a fraught experience for Liz. While Scott was quiet and bemused, Adam was openly hostile, angry and rude. Eventually Eddie moved in two days before Calum was born, much to Adam's disgust. In four years, relations between Eddie and Adam have remained difficult, while Eddie's relationship with Scott is at best amicable but distant. Liz is not particularly happy herself, feeling that despite changing partners, her quality of life remains low.

Liz's account of being a mother and caring for her three sons in this particular context is firmly structured around the concepts of discipline and control. Her descriptions of all three children centre primarily on their behaviour at home and at school, with particular emphasis placed on adult responsibility to tame the naturally unruly conduct of children. From Liz's perspective, children are wilfully agentic, but mischievous and irresponsible. She represents her sons as naturally fun-seeking with little sense of personal responsibility or orientation to the future. This undirected energy defines childhood for Liz and clearly separates children from adults. While children were represented as inevitably 'naughty', this misbehaviour was generally associated with an adult failure to control the situation. Although Liz views children as anarchic forces, she does not think they are capable of understanding the consequences of their actions. As a result they are dependent on adults for guidance and protection. Annette Lareau (2003) reports how working-class parents in her ethnographic study drew similar boundaries between child and adult. In these families children are told what to do, in contrast with middle-class households where reasoning strategies and negotiation are employed. Liz is aware of alternative values in terms of interacting with children, but she dismisses them as 'lovey, lovey' attitudes. School is an environment where she is particularly conscious of a different approach to dealing with children:

> And sometimes some of the teachers, they're, um, some of them round our school, I know it's nothing to do with the way you should be, but they don't act sometimes as though they're . . . Sometimes they are a bit too over-familiar with the children . . . They [children] think they can, you know, oh she's alright, you know we can do this and she won't say nothing. Whereas when I was at school you was the pupil and they was the teacher and whatever she said you did. Whereas now they're [teachers] frightened to upset them . . . As though they're, oh, you know, if they do something naughty, like we was, I don't know, sent outside the headmaster's room. And you had to sit and write lines or whatever . . . You know if they get a little bit too familiar with them it definitely don't do them no favours. They're not, they haven't got that strictness about them . . . You know, and it seems as though the children think they can do what they want. You know, oh, we're going to go and do some drawing. You know it's not as if, oh you're going to sit there, and you're going to sit and write numbers or something. If they don't want to do it they sort of like don't make them do it. And I think they should. Because as they get older they're going think, well, you know.

Much of Liz's account is taken up with descriptions of how she, as a mother, had coped with and checked her sons' conduct. These incidents are recounted with a full explanation of the possible catalysts for the 'naughtiness', a description of her appropriate response and an assurance that the behaviour had either ceased or was under control. She drew attention repeatedly to the essentially restrained, disciplined nature of her children's behaviour, and this was emphasised by the contrasts she regularly made between her own sons and other disobedient, out-of-control youngsters. Nevertheless, there was also an undercurrent of concern for the future running through Liz's account. Alongside her determination to keep her boys in line, she also expressed a fear of loosing control as they got older. This concern appeared to be associated with Liz's gendered understanding of what it means to mother boys. Liz views boys as particularly unruly and emphasised their strong will and their naturally boisterous temperament. From Liz's perspective, boys who are not brought up to respect and sometimes fear authority are likely to spiral out of control and become anti-social juvenile delinquents. She was acutely aware of prevailing public anxieties about anti-social behaviour and drew on media stories to illustrate her point about the importance of keeping children in line:

> Um, I just think it's the society of today, the children are, you know when you read on the news, read in the paper and listen on the news, the schools, they've just got no respect for the teachers . . . : Oh, I think I'd be absolutely heartbroken if my children were like that.
>
> So you think it's more about the fault of the teachers then?
>
> No, I do think it must stem from the home.
>
> Yeah?
>
> I do think it must stem from the home. Because if your child can do all these, you know, they go out, I mean I see that Ridings school, they was on the steps and the two teachers was walking up the and they were [sticks two fingers up, laughs].
>
> Well, some children do that to their parents, don't they?
>
> Yeah.
>
> So if you can do that to your mum and dad and they don't say nothing, well they can do it, think there's nothing wrong. I definitely think it starts at home.

Liz speaks from a position of conscious vulnerability here. Her older boys can be portrayed as coming from a broken home, they have a conflictual relationship with their stepfather and their class position marks them out as potential troublemakers. Middle-class parents can comment on such stories with a more comfortable detachment, in the knowledge that they refer to 'other' children. Yet Liz is determined not to be positioned as a bad parent and she draws on explicit examples to emphasise how she differs from those who are. She meets her perceived responsibility and controls her children, but the stakes are high, leaving little space to engage with the ideals of democratic parenting. Rather than cultivating her children as individuals she is more concerned to curb their self-seeking tendencies.

Although she has relatively traditional views about family life, Liz is not prepared to accept that living in a stepfamily places her boys at greater risk of (in her words) 'going off the rails'. Despite the bad press often given to stepfamilies, Liz was keen to explain the advantages of her particular family arrangement. She emphasised how the older boys have both their own father to maintain discipline and the (albeit distant) spectre of Eddie to ensure they never step too far out of line:

> 'Cos Eddie is quite strict. He wouldn't let them, even if they was friendly and talking and all that. You know he's quite strict with Calum really, and, um, I must admit though that Adam wouldn't ever answer me back in front of Eddie. And I do think that perhaps if I was on my own Adam would try and push a little bit more. And he knows now that Eddie's not going to put up with him speaking, not that he ever really does, but now and again he has answered me back and Eddie has to bite his tongue 'cos he doesn't want to cause a row. But he has said to me if I ever hear him speak like that I'm going to tell him. And I do say to Adam, if you speak like that Eddie will have to have words, and oh, he muttered under his breath something! And I think he is wary, because they're very, very rarely naughty when he's here. So he definitely does have some influence over them, 'cos they are wary.

From Liz's point of view, Eddie exerts a disciplining influence over Adam simply by living in the same household. To some extent she regards the poor relationship between Adam and Eddie as heightening this deterrent effect, raising the stakes on the consequences of conflict. Nevertheless, Liz also fears the repercussions of Eddie becoming practically involved with disciplining Adam or Scott, feeling that it would upset a delicate balance and possibly result in her sons' leaving to live with their father. The constraining effect that Liz claims Eddie has on her sons' behaviour was also applied to Pete, as a largely absent father. Liz explained how threatening to 'tell dad' improved Scott's behaviour at school:

> And I do say to them, I'll be telling your dad, you know when Ad-, Scott was a bit naughty. And I did tell him and he got a real telling-off. And I was telling him off about it and saying to him, if you don't want to learn and you're not going to get on. And the teacher's just going to think you're a pest and whatever class you go in you're just going to be labelled all the time. And then each Friday, for about four Fridays, I just went to see her and you know, she said like, oh he's made a good improvement. And I think knowing that I was going to tell his dad did help him knuckle down. And from that day to this I've not had any problems, I mean it was only a period of a couple of months. And that was when they had that young teacher from college and I just don't think there was the discipline there.

Despite these visits to the school and her efforts to reason with Scott, Liz is happy to attribute the improvement in her son's behaviour to his fathers influence, suggesting that the desire to avoid another 'real telling-off' led Scott to amend his efforts at school. The power and authority that Liz invests in fatherhood is central to her understanding of good parenting. Even though she undertakes most of the discipline in the house, the symbolic role of the strict father is crucial in her eyes. Force and coercion are viewed as necessary to childrearing to make sure that children conform to values and codes of conduct that will ultimately benefit them in the long run. Failing to ensure that children learn how to fit in is interpreted by Liz as a serious neglect, leading to future problems for the child and the parents. She explained that while her sons are kept in line and remain respectfully wary of their fathers, other children are allowed to run wild:

> But it may go four, five months. You know it's not as if every day they're getting a smack. Because after a little while that don't work, does it? It just makes them violent. But, um, they've got to be wary and they've got to have respect. You know, you hear children saying, oh why don't you shut up. You know, how can you speak to your parents like that? I think years ago our mums were stricter, and especially dads

> I think. I think the dads now have gone to pot . . . You know they have you know whereas, OK you could always get away with a little bit more with your mum, but the dad always had that air of authority, a little bit, um. But the dads now just seem like wimps. I don't know whether they're having them too young and they're not, they don't seem as if the majority have got any backbone. You know and they've got these 16, 17-year-olds throwing petrol bombs. Well you know, where is the dad?

Liz's discussion of the wimpish nature of many fathers draws heavily on media (and government) representations of out-of-control youngsters and their irresponsible parents. In the interview, Liz outlined a number of examples of unruly children, taken from daytime television programmes and the newspapers, to demonstrate the consequences of parents not exercising appropriate authority. She is able to navigate a minefield of negative, blaming press to selectively position herself as a sensible, competent and caring mother, primarily by arguing that her family circumstances enhance rather than undermine child development. This involves actively resisting many dominant discourses around 'sensitive mothering' and democratic parenting. Rather than appropriating developmental constructions of the child as a fragile, emerging individual whose potential is dependent on sensitive engagement with its parents, Liz draws on an (albeit gendered) view of boys as robust and boisterous. The child-centred approach advocated in developmental texts and many parenting classes is dismissed by Liz as over-indulgent ('lovey, lovey'), and is associated with the dysfunctional development it purports to insure against.

For Liz, encouraging and cultivating the individuality of her sons would make little sense given their vulnerability to being interpreted as dangerously uncontained. Also, as Annette Lareau (2003) and Walkerdine *et al.* (2001) note, the middle-class focus on equipping children with reasoning and negotiation skills can lead them to challenge or reject the authority of parents. Defiant middle-class children might be viewed as naturally struggling towards independence, but similarly disobedient working-class children (particularly boys) are likely to be constructed as a serious threat to society. This is highly racialised as well as classed and gendered. The behaviour of working-class black boys tends to elicit the most public concern, but recurring waves of hysteria about anti-social behaviour encompasses working-class youths across ethnicities. Parents of these children have become folk-devils, portrayed as uncaring and wilfully neglectful. This is the broader social context in which Liz seeks to raise her sons. Rather than facilitating their individuality, she is more exercised by the need to keep them in line for their and her own good.

Liz and motherhood – keeping them on the rails

The meaning that Liz attributes to mothering is to a large extent associated with remaining in control and steering her children towards a respectable future. As a result she views parenting in terms of an ongoing battle to keep children on the straight and narrow. A major concern for Liz is the potential corruptibly of her boys. She portrays them as naive, vulnerable and at risk of being drawn in with a 'bad crowd'. Consequently Liz sees a two-fold role for herself as a mother: she seeks to control her children's behaviour through surveillance and discipline, while also protecting them from bad influences. Her efforts to avoid her children being singled-out involve ensuring that they fit in with the mainstream. This requires her to monitor their whereabouts and keep her informed about their lives outside of the home. She was particularly keen to demonstrate her control over and knowledge of what her children are up to. For example, she described how Adam will always ring and ask permission before going anywhere after school:

> He'll never think, oh tough luck I'm not getting back. You know some of my friend's children, you know they won't ring . . . So I mean he wanted to go to Wolton last night, shopping. He'll always ring first, soon as he comes out of school and say can I go. He wouldn't just go and then come back, because he knows that I would really go mad. And I think he must be wary. I don't want them to be frightened of me but I want them to have a little bit of respect, that they wouldn't just wander off and be, I mean, he didn't come home till ten past five which, if he hadn't have told me, I'd have been frantic, because he finishes school at quarter past three . . . I know you've got to give them a little bit of leeway but, um, I wouldn't let them go out late at night. I mean I opened the door the other night and there was this little tot like this, um, trick or treat. You know it was about 8 o'clock and I though, what an earth is wrong with the mother? You know he was with his older brother but he was only about nine. To walk in the dark, I mean someone could just pick them up and run off with them, you wouldn't hear them. I think, oh I wouldn't let mine do that.

By emphasising Adam's respect, Liz conveys both her authority as parent and her success in bringing her son up to be considerate and well behaved. Both these points are reinforced by her initial comparison of Adam with the children of some of her friends. This distancing of herself from 'other' parents she knows occurs throughout Liz's account, and appears to represent an attempt to resist the negative positioning of her mothering practices. Through highlighting the perceived failings of other working-class mothers, she guards against misrecognition and seeks to demonstrate her knowledge of right and wrong. The 'other' mothers and their children are used as lightening rods to deflect attention while Liz stresses her grip on the situation. Singling out particular families allows Liz to occupy a more comfortable position as a normal, responsible parent.

Nevertheless, this exert reveals class-specific values around children's leisure time, suggesting that Liz's sons have considerably greater freedom compared with many of the middle-class children in the *Resources in Parenting* study. In line with Annette Lareau's (2003) ethnography of family life, we found middle-class parents often tightly structured children's spare time around after-school activities and supervised social events, leaving them little space to occupy themselves. This can, as Lareau suggests, be interpreted in terms of a conscious strategy of concerted cultivation of personal skills. Liz's primary concern, however, is to know that her sons are safe and under control. Her efforts to monitor the boys are associated with a more general commitment to full-time motherhood in terms of 'being there' if she's needed. For example, she explained how she oversees the movements of her children by staying close by and keeping an eye on them:

> I don't mind them playing out in the front, you know, and I can just look out and see them all. But you know, when they just say, oh we're just going up the road for a couple of hours, I want to know sort of who they're going with and where actually they are going to be going. And I've always been here so they've never had to be left on their own to fend for themselves or, they've never really, you know, got into mischief. You know, 'cos I've always been here.

Unlike many middle-class parents, Liz does not seek to ensure that her children's time is spent productively. A limited household income could not stretch to cover the often costly extra-curricular activities pursed by middle-class children. Furthermore, Liz does not have access to the 'right' kind of cultural capital to pass on through family activities. But her preoccupation with discipline reflects a deep concern for her sons' future lives. By keeping a tight reign on her children's conduct, she is expressing her emotional commitment to protecting their welfare, ensuring they are safe from the dangers associated with disorder and indiscipline. From Liz's perspective, lack of parental discipline derives from an emotional indifference to a child's wellbeing. Lax parents were portrayed as uncaring and irresponsible, failing to draw the necessary boundaries to protect their children. This perceived parental duty to ensure children conform and 'fit in' stems less from her desire to have obedient children and more from a fear for her boys if they don't 'knuckle under'. Although adhering to rules and respecting authority were highlighted as morally important, the consequences of stepping out of line were a more significant worry. For example, Liz explained how Adam is not able to risk 'messing about' at school because he invariably gets caught:

> I think he lacks concentration sometimes because he very easily, you know, if some other boy is sitting there flicking a pen he will turn round and laugh. And always get caught. He's not sort of like, um, very shrewd. I always say, if you're going to do something you've got to be a little bit more, you know. He's a very open boy.

Here, discipline appears less important to Liz than the chances of getting caught and she implies it is his naivety rather than his mischievous behaviour that is the problem. In contrast, his younger brother, Scott, is described as more astute to the potential negative consequences of being naughty. From Liz's point of view, being able to 'fit in' and live with rules and constraints is an essential part of life as an adult. Life is experienced and articulated as a struggle, and trying to exist outside an established social order of right and wrong is viewed by Liz as self-defeating, leading to condemnation and punishment. Liz is determined that her boys should do the best they can in a dangerous and difficult world, and this necessitates her protective, guiding influence as a mother. Part of this involves communicating a strong sense of the importance of 'knuckling under' and working within rather than against the system in order to survive. She was particularly concerned that 'mucking about' at school would damage future employment chances, as the following quote shows:

> Because if you don't come out of school without any qualifications you'll be stacking shelves at Tesco's. You just don't get a job do you . . . I think because I didn't do very well at school I want them to do well. Because I know that they're just, when I left school I mean I still got a job, and, um, it didn't affect me. But it does now because you didn't have to have qualifications then. You know so but, er . . .
>
> So you think they're more important now?

Oh, I think definitely, because there's so many people after the one job and they're not going to take someone who's done nothing or made trouble, they want someone who's, I mean, I don't expect him [Adam] to come back and say oh, you know I've got nine O-levels. You know, if he were just to get two or three.

Doing badly at school or being labelled as a troublemaker is regarded by Liz as a future albatross around the neck of anyone seeking a decent job. Her ambitions for Adam are relatively modest, but she outlines her strong desire for him to avoid leaving school without any qualifications. Notably she refers to the obsolete O-level rather than the current equivalent that Adam might gain (GCSEs). This suggests that she was drawing on her own personal experience of schooling at a time when the currency of O-levels was stronger. She does not expect him to do the impossible and get nine, but two or three is mentioned as enough to keep him in the mainstream. Unlike many middle-class parents, Liz does not see her son as having any special entitlement to academic success and can see no way that he would ever excel at school. There is little opportunity for her to change this lived reality. She cannot afford tutoring or private school, she has no teachers or educated professionals in her social network to draw inside knowledge from, and she has limited personal understanding of the cultural values and expectations structuring her sons' schools. In these circumstances the best Liz can hope for is for Adam to survive school as an average pupil. The worse-case scenario is that he is marked out as a failure or delinquent.

Liz's strong emphasis on discipline and 'knuckling under' was particular to her account, but a desire for children to be integrated rather than recognised as different was common to most of the mothers featured in this book. Having a 'special' child was more generally viewed as problematic, suggesting particular psychological or behaviour difficulties. Sally (the white working-class mother of seven children, discussed in Chapter 3) was a notable exception. Having undergone extensive counselling and training as a nursery nurse, Sally is fluent in the language of child-centred individual development. However, her experiences demonstrate that discourses of entitlement ring hollow without accompanying social and institutional legitimation.

Sally – nurturing potential

Sally's account of motherhood was striking in its theoretical and ideological consistency. Her insights closely resembled a humanistic model of childrearing, rather than the more general discussion of experiences and observations provided by the other mothers. It seemed that the counselling that she and her children had received after leaving her abusive first husband provided her with a highly structured and individualistic understanding of children's needs. This was reinforced and validated by the developmental psychology which structured her training to become a nursery worker. Children are presented by Sally as needing both space and flexibility to maximise their potential and develop without restraint or coercion. This emphasis on freedom and self-determination provides a strong contrast to Liz's alternative focus on discipline and control. Although Sally stressed the importance of knowing when to say 'no', and expressed confidence in her ability to prevent serious misbehaviour from her children, she is suspicious of methods of discipline employed by schools and other institutions. The rules and regulations enacted in her children's schools were viewed by Sally as overly rigid, causing serious problems for several of her sons.

Central to Sally's focus on nurturing her children's potential was her commitment to affirming their self-worth and increasing their confidence. References to the need for children to feel self-assured were made throughout the interview, combined with what appeared to be a consciously positive appraisal of each of her seven children as well as her stepdaughter. While the other mothers in this study discussed some of the difficulties and frustrations they faced in bringing up their sons or daughters, Sally carefully avoided labelling any behaviour or experience as problematic. It was conspicuous that any vaguely negative comment Sally made about her children was immediately qualified by an explanation and balanced by an additional description of a more positive trait. This emphasis reflects Sally's particular concern to pre-empt her children being put down or written off. Her role as a nurturer of her children's potential was driven by her deeply felt responsibility to provide them with encouragement and positive affirmation. She repeatedly stressed the importance of boosting a child's self-esteem and gave numerous examples of the ways in which she actively seeks to reinforce her own children's positive self-regard:

> And it's around things, making the child feel important. That they know their own self-worth. And that's why so often you get children with low self-esteem all the time. Because they don't believe in their own worth. And it's only by telling them how good they are and how important they are. And there are so many ways of doing it and it isn't all ways verbally. I mean just like a touch on the head, you know it's just you're aware of they're there. Their importance, you know, they know it.

This emphasis on self-esteem was very closely linked to the notion of developing as an individual. From Sally's point of view, children must feel valued in order to grow into their emerging personalities, and this positive self-perception can only be gained via reassurance from others (particularly parents). For Sally, recognising, encouraging and valuing her seven children as unique individuals is a vital task of motherhood. She explained how she consciously ensures that each child is recognised and appreciated, and how this requires the devotion of space and time as a mother. In particular she described the vulnerability of her youngest four boys:

> Because they're so close in age. 'Cos all four of them were born within a three and a half year span, and that has made it a bit crowded to find their place. So they need to be allowed to find their own role. And also to be reminded that they are special and given the space to develop as individuals. 'Cos they're often lumped together.

Sally sees herself as responsible for counteracting the negative effects that she associates with individuals being or becoming 'lumped together'. This perceived threat to individuality is identified as external, in the form of people generalising and comparing the boys, but also internal, in the form of stifled, overcrowded environments impairing the development of unique selves. As a family they cope with both of these conditions on a day-to-day basis. By seeking to make her boys feel 'special', Sally reinforces their status as worthy individuals, 'reminding' them that despite any experience to the contrary, they have separate highly valued identities. But implicit in Sally's emphasis on positive affirmation is her perceived need to protect her sons from a denial of their rights as individuals. Sally is resolutely determined to challenge negative interpretations by teachers and social workers, but is aware she has her work cut out in claiming their entitlements as selves. Her sense that her children's deservingness is often overlooked provokes anger and frustration in her, as is evident from the exchange below:

> So they're all quite different then?
>
> Well of course they are! Everybody has different personalities and I think it's important to treat them like that. And it's very easy to lump them all together and alright you're [pause] but then how do they develop as a person? And you have to treat each and every one of them differently. They're all different, they're their own person.

Probing her individualistic values in a less than sensitive way provoked one of several distinctly sharp responses from Sally during the interview. Perhaps understandably I was positioned as another of the many middle-class professionals who 'lumped' her children together and sought to deny them their individual humanity. Sally's anger was contained but evident throughout, and appeared to stem from her inability to secure not only appropriate recognition, but also accompanying resources. Several of her sons have been marked out as having behavioural difficulties, with Jamie (10) having been permanently excluded from his previous school. Sally feels she should have received more help from the school, and is particularly angry at the way Jamie was marginalised and ignored after he was excluded from school:

> Did you see anyone else, you know, when he was excluded did, was there any other contact with any other services?
>
> No, nothing.
>
> Do you think there should have been?
>
> Of course there should have been, and we tried very hard to get things for him but we didn't have a lot of luck. It was very bad because for someone who was so bad with his socialising one thing he didn't need to be was isolated. Yeah, we were let down there. It's like you get written off. It's like as long as he's not causing problems at school he doesn't matter, and of course that feeds right into his self-esteem problem and makes him feel even worse.

While she was clearly angry at the way Jamie had been neglected, Sally expressed very little surprise or outrage. Her expression 'you get written off' highlighted her strong sense of identification with her son as someone pushed to the margins and ignored. Her observation that as long as he's not causing problems at school he doesn't matter' suggests she felt Jamie was disregarded before his behaviour became defined as problematic. This is conveyed through a construction of the world as characteristically unjust. As well as describing the inevitable, largely unavoidable inequalities faced by her children, she drew on a concept of ingrained, inescapable unfairness to make sense of her own personal experience of frustration, disappointment and prejudice. Despite having access to a middle-class discourse of entitlement, Sally is relatively powerless to act on it. For example, she attributes Joel's troubles at school to the rigid and insufficiently flexible teachers:

He can play up, but then it's often because he's not being allowed to express himself. You know he's bright, intelligent, but with loads of energy and that can get directed towards mischief if he's not careful. I think he gets misunderstood, which is bad for his confidence and means he doesn't learn how to harness his potential, if you know what I mean.

How's he get on with the teachers?

Um, some very well, some not so well. Some his fault and some's theirs.

What's an example of things that may be at school?

Not doing as he's told [laughs] and there's, um, they don't listen, they say something and that's it, because they've said it that's it. It's ingrained in stone if you like, but there's no movement with them. There's no give. Whereas kids need a bit more leeway, you know. Sometimes it's better to be flexible and look at the situation rather than relying on all these rules that don't make no sense in reality. As far as certain teachers are concerned, there's never any reason for why Joel is doing something he shouldn't be.

Sally stresses the inability of teachers to cope with Joel's individuality and harness his potential, but is ultimately unable to change this in any way. In the *Resources in Parenting* study, the few middle-class mothers whose children were struggling at school employed strikingly similar explanations, but to very different effect. For example, Katherine (the white middle-class lone mother of two, discussed earlier in this chapter) experienced behavioural problems with Zoe, her eldest daughter. Zoe had been disruptive and violent in the classroom, yet unlike Sally, Katherine had been able to secure special attention for her daughter. Katherine drew on her considerable financial capital to commission a private specialist assessment of Zoe which concluded she was dyslexic, but with a very high IQ. Katherine then utilised this official diagnosis alongside her influential cultural and social capital to negotiate recognition, tolerance and extra help from the school. As a working-class mother of seven children from three different relationships, Sally would struggle to command anything like the same respect or influence from teachers as Katherine expects as a matter of course. As I will show in the next chapter, she is considerably more likely to be viewed as unreasonable, irrational and a troublemaker.

Conclusion: individualism and mothering

In this chapter I've attempted to show how understandings of self, other and child are profoundly classed. Although individualistic values structure contemporary society, they obscure the more relational experiences of the disadvantaged and marginalised. Working class mothers and their children are denied the recognition and resources to construct themselves as worthy subjects. Their resulting inability to cultivate 'acceptable' middle-class selves is then used to explain their disadvantage through personal as opposed to structural shortcomings. Yet standing outside of the middle-class project of the self generates values and dispositions that are commonly coverted and fetishised by contemporary Western governments. Working class mothers tend to live in tight-knit communities characterised by trust, obligation and mutual responsibility. Their more dispersed sense of self is conveyed through a highly developed sense of interdependency and loyalty.

Nevertheless, concerns about the moral dangers of rampant individualism primarily feature working-class families who are portrayed as atomised, disconnected and a threat to social cohesion. As Janet Finch (1994) notes, anxiety over the demise of working-class filial affection is evident from at least the nineteenth century, reflecting the reluctance of the wealthier classes to accept financial responsibility for the destitute. In the UK, policy rhetoric consistently cites the fracturing of traditional support systems and a decline in values of duty and responsibility as a justification for intervening in working-class family life (Edwards and Gillies 2004; Gillies 2005a). This highlights a fundamental contradiction, with working-class mothers represented as both selfish and inappropriately individualised. I have sought to demonstrate through this chapter that they are neither.

The mothers in this book gain little advantage through asserting the unique individuality of their children. Their only institutionally sanctioned way of claiming such exceptionality it through severe failure or misconduct, and like Liz most sought to avoid this at all costs. Middle-class parents, however, rely on underperforming or average working-class children to claim greater entitlement for their children on the grounds of their natural superiority. Analysis of the middle-class interviews in the *Resources in Parenting* project revealed how children like Adam (Liz's son) and Jamie (Sally's son) are regularly cited to highlight contrasting potential and deservingness (see Gillies 2005b). The social, cultural and material resources underpinning children's development are made conveniently invisible through a moral emphasis on aptitude and merit.

The example of Sally illustrates the empty nature of entitlement claims without social recognition. Despite a prevailing focus on the importance of self-esteem and aspiration for children in UK policy literature, Sally's assertions about the unique individuality and worthiness of her children bring few benefits. More often than not they set her on a collision course with an education system designed promote and value middle-class attributes. Mothers that lack sanctioned middle-class cultural capital struggle to exert power or influence in such institutional arenas. This does not stop them fighting hard when they feel their children are being mistreated, but as I will show in the next chapter the situations they find themselves in may necessitate direct and extreme battle strategies.

Chapter 5

Challenging from the margins

Managing institutional frameworks

In this chapter I will explore how working-class mothers handle the formal, institutional areas of their children's lives. More specifically the focus is on interactions with teachers, and other middle-class professionals who exert power over the day-to-day lives of families. I begin by examining classed understandings of public private boundaries. I show how the concept of home holds a particular significance for working-class mothers, given their experience of external and institutional spaces as hostile, ruthless environments populated by dangerous people. Home life in middle-class families more often than not blends with school and other formal activities. In contrast, working-class families are more likely to view children as inhabiting very separate worlds inside and outside of school. Working class mothering is primarily situated in the home and is often misinterpreted and devalued in professional arenas, particularly in the context of education. Using case study examples I will show how such institutional interactions are interpreted and managed by the mothers in this book.

Where possible the mothers avoided contact with institutions and they interpreted lack of communication with teachers as a sign that their children were progressing satisfactorily. As a result, dealings with education professionals were primarily associated with a child's bad behaviour, academic problems or experiences of bullying. These encounters were usually fraught, characterised by a cultural clash of expectations and values. During visits to headteachers' offices, the mothers often felt disrespected and ignored, and this could force them to adopt a more determined stance in order to fight for their children's rights. Drawing on the example of Nina, a white working-class mother, I will show how attitudes and actions that might be read by professionals as unreasonable or aggressive are grounded in a prevailing power imbalance. Issues of race can also interact with class and gender in shaping conflicts with professionals, as the second case study example of Juile, an African-Caribbean mother, illustrates. An exploration of such disputes from the perspective working-class mothers highlights the profound gap between professional assumptions and lived experience.

Parenting and the significance of home

For the mothers in this research, family life is primarily conducted behind closed doors. Running across their accounts was a strong construction of the world as a hazardous, brutal place, and of their personal position as fragile and exposed. Most lived in areas considered as underprivileged and this entailed coping with poor housing, lack of facilities and a high crime rate. The mothers made a clear distinction between outside and inside in terms of what constituted their home or family life, and what represented the external world they and their children were forced to negotiate. While home was portrayed as a safe, nurturing place, outside environments were perceived as being 'dog eat dog', populated by ruthless, mercenary people. The more relational experience of self discussed in the last chapter was partly maintained through a strong construction of 'them and us'. The importance of close friends and family was heightened by experiences of a harsh and often treacherous world.

Most of the mothers conveyed a sense of feeling under siege from various risks and hazards, and emphasised their constant need to remain vigilant and wary. Almost all had encountered physical violence against themselves or their children. Although this occurred in the street, housing estate and school playground, violence could also penetrate the home in the form of domestic disputes. Like Sam (discussed in Chapter 3), Sally (discussed in Chapter 4) and Kelly (discussed later on in this chapter), many of the mothers fought hard to escape this threat by building new and safe homes. For the most part home was experienced as a haven from the demanding and risky social life characterising day-to-day encounters.

The mothers' perception of the world as dangerous and hostile was particularly stressed in relation to their children's need to become streetwise and socially competent. The mothers expressed a great deal of anxiety about their children's encounters with people outside of the home, such as other children, teachers and some neighbours. Children are viewed as vulnerable to bullying and intimidation and concerted efforts were often made by the mothers to toughen them up. Home is the site where mothers provided their children with the emotional resources to deal with the outside world. This could involve bolstering assertiveness and self-defence skills. For example, Sam (the white lone mother discussed in Chapter 3) described how she encouraged her daughter (Sophie) to stand up for herself at school when she encountered a bully:

Well, they [the school] said that 'cos this little girl . . . was French she can't understand English very much and she gets very frustrated and she ends up hitting the children. So I said alright, so she [teacher] said

> that's why and I said is anything going to be done about it, so she said well nothing really can be done about it really. So now she's getting, um, the teacher's like nothing really can be done about it. So I said oh well, if she's getting frustrated because she can't speak English, Sophie's going to get frustrated and smack her back 'cos she hates being smacked, and that's when they started doing things about it. But, um, so I said to Sophie, hit her back and make sure you do it properly.

The ability to fight back against bullying and abuse was regarded as vital, and Sam described how she had become alarmed at Sophie's passive response to this domineering and violent child. Sam did not seem particularly surprised that her initial complaints to the teacher were so ineffectual and she could see little mileage pursuing the issue any further with the school. Her instruction to Sophie to hit the French girl back was presented as a reasonable response to protect her daughter against further abuse. Telling her to 'do it properly' emphasises the purpose of the act, to secure a deserved basic freedom from harm.

Sam's experience of a teacher who is unwilling to validate and protect her daughter's rights reflects a more general sense from working-class mothers that their children are not valued in the classroom. The emphasis on attainment and intelligence means that other personal virtues can be overlooked or underappreciated. For example, Denise's son Liam is struggling at school and is receiving extra help from his class teachers to bring his literacy level up. While he is labelled as failing at school, Denise is keen to emphasise Liam's non-academic qualities of likeability and good behaviour:

> I mean I'm not blowing me own trumpet, but I get complimented on how he is with people, so that's a good thing for yourself, it boosts you. . . . I've been lucky that I've had a gooden.

But this sense of pride represents an alternative value system that can best be articulated outside of school. In school Liam is a problem, a slow learner with particularly poor literacy skills. Outside of school he is a kind, polite and good kid. For many working-class mothers, disengagement from their children's school is a way of ensuring that their children's worth is recognised (Gillies 2006a, 2006b). Direct involvement with teachers was often associated with children getting in trouble, and consequently the school could be viewed as a hostile, dangerous world in which children were successful if they avoided attention from the teachers. As will be outlined in Chapter 6, emotional resources in the form of love, support and positive connotation are often communicated by working-class mothers as part of a prioritisation of home, particularly in the context of school failure.

Home-school boundaries

As Carol Vincent (2000) notes, parenting and family life is increasingly presented as an 'educational project' to be worked at. Involvement in a child's school life is viewed as an essential component of good parenting. Yet as Vincent points out, it remains unclear what the purpose and role of such involvement should be. For middle-class families there are clear cultural commonalities linking home and school. Middle-class children often move seamlessly between the two arenas, with leisure time and education merging through after school activities and 'quality time' spent with parents (Lareau 2003). For working-class families, however, school can be experienced as a dislocation, with many aspects of working-class culture routinely devalued and disrespected. The mothers in my research wanted their children to do well at school (and as I will show in the next chapter, they made important educational contributions), but they were unable to pursue middle-class concerted cultivation techniques. Instead they relied in the main on schools to educate their children and stressed the responsibility of teachers. For example, Louise, a white working-class mother, articulates a moral and practical reason for why too much should not be expected of parents:

Do you get involved? [with the school]

Much as I can, er, I try and do a lot with them at home but again it's a time factor . . . just don't get as much done as we would want to do, you know you shouldn't really be doing as much as they are in the classroom, at home anyway, you know I don't think I should be having to help Lucy you know . . . parents do suffer with dyslexia and, you know, reading and literacy problems and then of course they can't help the children at home so . . . it just has a knock-on effect really.

So you feel there is too much emphasis really on parents?

Yes. Because you know you shouldn't have to be, you know they're there to be taught at school and that's what should happen, but you know far too much emphasis is put now on parents to help a lot more at home than they should be doing but . . .

So you do what you can.

Yeah, I do what I can. And not only that, she doesn't want to do it when she comes home, she's at school all day and you know I can understand where she's coming from when she . . . she wouldn't want to sit there for two hours, you know, scribbling to . . . because it doesn't help her in the end because she's not taking it in, she's tired herself and, er . . . sometimes you just think it has an adverse effect and make them go even more backward then.

Reflecting the dominant expectations surrounding parental involvement in education, Louise initially focuses on lack of time to justify her limited interventions at home. More substantial, though, is her sense that she should not be expected to act as an educator as this merely compounds a cycle of disadvantage. This view is combined with a belief that home is a necessary sanctuary from the rigours of school. The separation between home and school makes absolute sense to working-class mothers because the two arenas serve very different purposes for their children. In the home children are cared for and loved by their parents and are sent out to school to be educated. The mothers do not regard childhood as a developmental project in the same way as many middle-class parents. They do not have the same easy familiarity with educational concepts and values and often struggle to understand the work brought home by their children. They have a limited amount to offer their children as educators, but as mothers they are able to support them through the culture shock of adjusting to the school environment. As I will show in Chapter 6, working-class mothers' efforts are often directed towards ensuring their children survive school without being emotionally crushed.

Boundaries between home and school are often enforced by children themselves (Edwards and Alldred 2000). Attempts by working-class mothers to become more involved in their children's school lives can be met with fierce resistance by their children. For middle-class mothers in the *Resources in Parenting* study, helping their children complete homework sheets or discussing their latest set reading book was often experienced as a cosy, intimate point of connection for the family. For the working-class mothers in this book it was more likely to represent a site of conflict, uncertainty and vulnerability. Nevertheless, working-class mothers do cross the home–school boundary when they feel it is necessary. Unlike the middle-class parents in the *Resources in Parenting* study who assume a role in monitoring and regulating school activities, working-class mothers were most likely to step in and argue on behalf of their children when accusations of bad behaviour or exceptionally poor academic standards were made to them by teachers. In contrast, the middle-class parents were more inclined to identify problems themselves and intervene if they felt their children were being held back or not given sufficient credit.

Most of the working-class mothers in this book expressed a strong emotional commitment to challenging vigorously any potential victimisation of their children by teachers. This was particularly evident in the *Resources in Parenting* study where parents were asked what they would do if their child came home from school complaining that a teacher was picking on them. While the answers given by middle-class parents were generally conciliatory, suggesting they would assume a mediating role when talking to teachers, working-class parents were more likely to envisage an acrimonious encounter. This needs to be seen in the context of a prevailing balance of power. Such parents are often painfully aware that in the school environment they are positioned as problematic and inferior, and as a result can feel they have little alternative but to fight hard. Also for many working-class parents conflict is a defining feature of life, shaping a day-to-day struggle to get by. As the case study example of Nina demonstrates, basic rights and recognition may have to be fought for continually, provoking a battle-hardened and sometimes confrontational approach to professionals.

Nina – fighting for rights

Nina is a white lone mother and lives with her 10-year-old daughter in a council flat on an estate in a densely populated urban area. She described how she had become pregnant while in an on–off relationship with Bill, a man considerably older than herself. Bill already had two children from his first marriage and several others from less permanent relationships, the details of which Nina was unclear about. Nina stated that although Amy had not been deliberately planned, having a baby had not been consciously ruled out either. She explained that she had risked having unprotected sex several times. Reflecting back on it now, she feels she had an unconscious desire to have baby. At the time of her pregnancy, Nina was living in council flat in a tower block with her best friend Monica and Monica's boyfriend. Bill also moved in at this time, while Nina applied to the council for her own flat.

For Nina becoming a mother was experienced in terms of an ongoing battle. This began with Amy's birth, which she describes in terms of being misled by medical staff, labelled as a troublemaker and discriminated against. On returning home with Amy, Nina was offered her own council flat on a notoriously grim estate with a reputation for violent crime and drugs. She reluctantly accepted and lived there with Bill and Amy for nearly three years, 'hating every moment of it'. Eventually Nina met another mother who was prepared to swap her council tenancy on a more desirable estate, for payment. Nina described how this period of her life was particularly stressful, emphasising her desperation to move. Having finally signed the contracts, Bill disappeared. Nina was left to arrange the move at short notice by herself, with only the help of Bill's sister, who also needed somewhere to live. After a few months Bill's sister moved out and Bill eventually moved back in, although he still often disappeared for weeks at a time. She described how he would 'go out to buy a paper, but not say what date'. When he was around Nina felt he 'took over' the flat, making decisions about how it should be decorated and taking up too much space in the wardrobe. She gradually realised that she was beginning to look forward to Bill's regular disappearances.

Nina also discussed Bill's drinking binges, violent temper and his lack of humour. She described how during this time she had insisted on Bill sleeping on the settee, and had stopped any sexual relationship with him. This arrangement came to an abrupt end when he 'started on her' one night. She described how she had to run out of the flat and call the police to have him removed. From then on he visited only infrequently to see Amy. Nina explained how Amy and Bill had a good relationship, when he was around, but his prolonged absences and lack of commitment took its toll. Nina found Bill's occasional interventions as a parent undermining and unhelpful, and felt they were disturbing for Amy. Although Nina did not actively stop Bill seeing Amy, his visits gradually ceased over time.

Vulnerability, power and control are particularly prominent themes in Nina's account, articulated through her description of an ongoing struggle to secure basic rights for herself and her daughter. The hostile, prejudiced world in which people struggle to live is seen by Nina as constituting childhood in just the same way that it does adulthood. For Nina, there is no protective buffer zone separating the harsh realities of adult life from the vulnerability of childhood. In spite of the power differential children are seen as fellow fighters, and sometimes as active adversaries. Nina described bringing up her daughter as if it were a war of attrition, emphasising her continual battle to maintain some authority. Like Liz (discussed in Chapter 4), Nina regarded protection and control to be primary features of a mother's role, but while Nina is confident of her competence in fighting for Amy, she feels considerably less successful when engaging in mother–daughter power struggles. Although Nina acknowledged her power and influence as a parent, she also stressed Amy's ability to fight back and wield significant power of her own. As well as directly defying her mother, Amy was portrayed as manipulating situations and people in order to achieve her goals. According to Nina, Amy was also prone to loosing her temper and erupting in tantrums, forcing her mother to act in one way or another. The following quote details one of the many fraught encounters described in Nina's account and demonstrates the power that she attributes to Amy:

We had a row over peanut butter sandwiches. Because she wouldn't get out the kitchen. And I said get out the kitchen, I didn't like her in the kitchen.

How old was she then?

She was still three, coming up to four then . . . And she wouldn't get out the kitchen, I didn't like her in the kitchen 'cos she, I mean she was only, you know, a toddler and all that. And I didn't want her in the kitchen because of accidents and everything like that. 'Get out the kitchen'. 'No I'm not getting out of the kitchen.' I said 'right, I'm not making you sandwiches.' And that was it, she just got everything and she just, she just threw it all over the place. I think she must have been coming up near four then. And I said 'right, that is it' and I put her pyjamas on, and the screams of her! She hadn't had a smack or anything like this. It was sheer temper. It was stubbornness on my part. I was not going to smack her. I was not going to give in to her. Um, but she was not going to, you know, display this bloody behaviour. And then the neighbours started coming up and started having a go. I mean, I suppose to them they must have thought there was something going on . . . But there was nothing other than this was a child's tantrum. And boy would she have tantrums. And he [Bill] came up and that was it – 'WHAT THE FUCK DO YOU WANT' – 'I've come to return her coat' – 'OUT OF MY FUCKING HOUSE'. And we had this great big row and all this lot. And the neighbours called the police and everything like that. So the police sort of like came up and they sort of like, saying to me, you shouldn't shout at the child and you shouldn't shout in front of the child. You know, I said 'what are you giving me all this bollocks for, you're out at work all day you're not bringing up your children, your wife is'.

Amy's power to cause havoc is clearly communicated in this extract, along with Nina's struggle to gain some authority over her daughter. Amy's refusal to leave the kitchen is identified as the origin of a specific power struggle that spiralled well out of Nina's (and Amy's) control, involving Bill, neighbours and the police. But while Amy was the initial source of the problem, Nina's anger was plainly focused on the others who became involved. Nina presented her struggle to maintain control over her daughter as a necessary duty of motherhood, made particularly difficult by Amy's wilful, obstinate nature. She then shifts from describing a battle of wills with Amy, to explaining how she fought off an attack undermining the best interests of herself and her daughter. Nina's account of mother–daughter power struggles are invariably contextualised by this wider and more critical battle for rights.

Nina's fight against this outside intervention is presented as a reasonable response to being misinterpreted and attacked unfairly by neighbours and police who were described as 'having a go'. Her furious response to being told what she should and shouldn't do in a situation she was attempting to control was compounded by this strong sense of injustice. Significantly the policeman was accused of having little practical commitment to his own children, and therefore no moral right to interfere in Nina's parenting. This sense that professionals do not have the entitlement to dispense parenting advice was shared by numerous mothers in the research. As I will explore in the next chapter, most felt they were making a good job of raising their children in difficult and demanding circumstances. Interventions from professionals were commonly viewed as naive and based on theory rather than experience, as the following quote from Paula illustrates:

> Aye, I wouldn't go for advice, because half of them don't know what they are speaking about anyway. It's like half of that district nurses, I mean they have not got bairns so how can they read it out of a text book; the text book is a load of rubbish! [Laughter] . . . When the kids were little, they tell you to do this and do that and do the next thing and you think, how do you know?

Many of the mothers sought to deal diplomatically with this kind interference from professionals by humouring them but ultimately ignoring their advice, as Denise explains:

> Me mum were alive then, bless her, and she used to say, tell them what they want to hear Denise, but you do what works. So I used to go in and she [health visitor] used to say 'You're not giving him rusks, are you?' I'd say no, he's just on milk, Pam. I'd come home and give him a rusk to settle him at night and that were. She did everything by the book, she had no kids of her own.

However, Nina was often unable to contain her anger at professionals and institutions which she often perceived to be acting out of malice or 'laziness'.

At the centre of her account of life as an ongoing battle is a strong notion of morality and justice. The clear distinction she makes between right and wrong and the emphasis she places on moral judgement provides her with an important focus to make sense of the world, and this drives her struggle against unfair treatment. She often feels deliberately targeted and denied rights by people who are abusing their power, and this has left her with a sense of needing to be constantly on her guard to fight against the mistreatment and discrimination that has so far characterised her life.

Vulnerability and power – fighting back

Nina's evaluation of the world as ruthless and corrupt invokes an instinctive suspicion and antagonism towards institutions and individuals with authority. She gives several examples of the way she had been misled by doctors, nurses, teachers and council officials, but Nina appears to derive considerable strength and resilience from the anger this provokes. Although she foregrounds her vulnerability in this portrayal of herself as under attack, ultimately it is her power that is emphasised. Nina's interview is full of detailed descriptions of the way she and Amy have been subjected to misinformation, misrepresentation and inequity. There are also passionate descriptions of the battles she has fought and won over the years, on behalf of herself and her daughter. Unlike most of the other mothers in this research, Nina has a keen sense of her own oppression. This is experienced as a powerful insight which enables her to fight, rather than submit to an established order. Consequently, despite her overall focus on injustice, Nina is anxious to avoid positioning either herself or her daughter as passive victims. Both are presented as actively fighting for their rights in an arena in which the odds are stacked against them. Nina, in particular, portrays herself as shrewd and perceptive, a representation that is partly conveyed through a conscious acknowledgement of her vulnerability and need to keep fighting.

Nina's interpretation of encounters with institutions is notably focused on power dynamics and the motives and manoeuvres of those concerned. She emphasised the cynical, untrustworthy nature of people, and the need to remain vigilant and expect the worst. She also described how, when faced with unreasonable or threatening behaviour, she fights back, determined not to be abused or wronged. Although this combative stance is at times aggressive and antagonistic, her approach needs to be understood in the context of her life as a marginalised lone mother. Many of the battles Nina describes are over basic resources such as money, housing and safety in terms of freedom from violence. Nina cannot afford to lose such battles, and the intensity of her responses often reflect the significance of what is at stake.

For example, she described the struggle she engaged in with the Department of Social Security to receive benefits and grants, while keeping Bill's presence secret. She also discussed the conflicts and threats that were encountered on a day-to-day basis. This struggle for survival ranged from dealing with aggressive neighbours, protecting possessions from known burglars, and even battling against an infestation of mice in the flat. Nina plainly experienced and accepted conflict as a central part of her life, and was resigned to being ruthless at times. For example, the prospect of exchanging her council flat and moving off of the notorious 'Atwood' estate inspired a hard-nosed determination in Nina when she heard that someone in a better area might be prepared to swap:

And then I'd heard about, the rumour came to me that Ann, what's her name, Ann Marshall. That was it, Ann Marshall, who's sister I had a fight with over the pool table. Amy was over Bill's sister's. And Karen [Bill's sister] was the one who was able to talk money. You know, 'Offer that girl ex amount or a hundred pound, when she goes give her nothing.' So I said I can't not give her nothing, but I said can you chat her up, 'cos I will give her some money, but I won't [pause]. So we would go round there and Karen would chat her up and you'd see the old pound signs in the eyes. And it was going to be near to a very good pub and near to her mum and every thing like that. And 'Ann, we'll give you, we'll bung you a couple of bob' and all this lot. And we started off at 200. I didn't say 200 but we sort of like intimated it could be sort of like 200 and I'd pay for the removals, and I was getting really psyched up. I was moving at last. Nobody ever gets off the Atwood except in a hardboard box and all that lot. And then a week or two before moving, Sue, that was it Sue Grant, who's one lady you do not muck about with. She was walking past the, er, her flat one day and she said 'Oh Ni', she goes, 'I hear Ann's not going to move'. 'DO WHAT?' So she actually, I think she was egging for a fight . . . She wanted me to have a fight with Ann. Well, there was no way I was going to do that. You know I couldn't do that. But I went round looking for her to try and sort this out. 'Cos the rumour according to Sue was that her sister and her mum were saying don't move on to the Atwood. But I couldn't find her. Luckily I couldn't find her, 'cos she heard that I was looking for her and she came up. She came up the next day and by that time I was at temper point and I thought, 'cos I was so desperate to get off the Atwood, I thought if she says to me no I'm not moving I would hit her at that point. But the day before couldn't have. I'm not that calculated. So she came up and went 'Oh, I am gonna move, I am gonna move'. So right, right, OK, we did move and I paid for all the removals and I bunged her a hundred quid. So I kept my deal and she's still on there. But she seems alright there. She seems happy. I mean, she was giving the neighbours hell here. I mean, she was having God knows who up and music blaring. And she was driving the neighbours absolutely potty here. So for a while I was a godsend to them, till they found out I was a single parent. But when I moved . . . 'Cos I wasn't satisfied until we actually signed those contracts. And I took Ann up and made her meet me. Took her up to sign those contracts, 'cos all she was thinking was money, money, money. And all I was thinking was, get off this estate, you know.

Nina's description of the process of agreeing and finalising the details of the exchange highlights her perceived need to fight hard in order to move forward. Efforts to convince Ann Marshall to exchange centred at first on verbal persuasion, offering money and pointing out the benefits of moving, but the undertones of physical coercion are implied throughout, and are explicitly referenced at times. From the beginning of this story, Ann Marshall is identified as someone 'who's sister I had a fight with over the pool table', highlighting their previous history of physical conflict. Sue Grant's attempt to provoke a fight between Nina and Ann is then depicted as a further dimension to the struggle, upping the ante and introducing a heightened friction to events. Nina's determination to move is presented as central to this struggle to move, spurring on her battle to secure the exchange. The extent of her desperation is clear and emphasised by her admission that she would have hit Ann if she had backed out.

While Nina's efforts to get off the Atwood are striking in terms of their brutal determination, her actions are no less ruthless than those engaged in by many middle-class parents in their efforts to ensure their children retain their existing advantage (see Reay 2005b; Ball 2003). Nevertheless, in her description of the negotiations surrounding the move, Nina carefully justifies her actions in moral terms. Although the gist of the story concerns Nina's successful attempt to coerce and bully another mother into exchanging her council flat for one on a notoriously grim estate, her own integrity and reasonable nature is stressed throughout. First, she distances herself from the initial idea, describing how Bill's sister took a lead in 'talking money' and 'chatting up' Ann. Then she explains how she firmly rejected Bill's sister's suggestion that she offer the money but not pay up. While she acknowledges that a higher sum than was actually paid may have been casually 'intimated', the fact that Nina 'kept her deal' was emphasised as an honourable action. Nina also warrants her actions by discussing how Ann's need for money corresponded with her own need to move. Ann was described as having 'pound signs' in her eyes and was portrayed as willingly entering into the exchange for her own benefit. Nina also appeared to undermine Ann's moral right to remain in her original flat, suggesting she had 'given the neighbours hell' before she moved. Nina was also keen to stress that Ann seemed happy on the Atwood estate, thus vindicating, to some extent, the pressure that Nina had placed her under.

Nina's ability to explain her actions within a moral framework contextualises her overarching construction of her life as a battle. Accounts of her fights with institutions and organisations are fuelled by a powerful sense of injustice. For example, Nina described how she struggled to get council housing while she was pregnant with Amy:

> And I applied for council housing and they were sort of like being shits saying no I'm not going to house you and all this lot. So I was living there and about six weeks later they made me an offer. I think they got a bit scared because I went in with a threatened miscarriage, and she came four weeks early. And I think they got a bit scared. Er, Vernon was her name, venomous Vernon. Um, as she's known as. And, um, she was only a housing allocations assistant but now she's, well, she was like head of housing. That's what you get for being a venomous little bitch. But she wouldn't come down to meet me, she sent down her little sidekick. But I think by that time they were running a bit scared. And the medical officer got involved and liased on my case. She even actually said to Mel [Nina's friend] 'You know you could if you want to, if you feel aggrieved, just actually put in a complaint'.

Nina clearly felt personally discriminated against in this situation, interpreting Vernon's initial refusal to house her as an attack motivated by spite or 'venom'. The unreasonable actions of the housing assistant are presented as a malicious abuse of power, denying Nina's right to a council flat despite her obvious need. Her description of the housing assistant and her 'sidekick' 'running scared' underlines their violation of authority, constructing them as consciously aware of the unprincipled nature of their actions. The medical officer's suggestion that a complaint could be lodged is presented as a further vindication of Nina's fight against the corrupt behaviour of the housing assistant. Hence the narrative of this story concerns the way the housing officer and her sidekick were forced to back down from their victimisation of Nina when faced with the prospect that their actions might rebound against them.

Apart from the overall satisfaction of justice prevailing in a largely unjust world (with this injustice symbolised by the housing officer's subsequent promotion to head of housing), Nina conveys a strong sense of her power to challenge discrimination through confrontation. Her account of this struggle with the housing department is notable in the way it portrays them as vulnerable and exposed. Vernon is described as 'only a housing allocations assistant', while both Vernon and the sidekick are referred to a 'little' ('little bitch' and 'little sidekick'). Their 'scared' reaction to the involvement of the medical officer further emphasises their precarious position in attempting to block Nina's right to obtain a flat. The emphasis Nina places on her power and assertiveness in this story to some extent underplays the vulnerable predicament she was in. Pregnant, homeless and facing a real possibility of miscarriage, this was a fight Nina could not afford to lose.

Other mothers in the research also found they needed to fight to avoid being ignored or discriminated against, particularly in their dealings with their children's school. However, Nina was exceptionally dogged in such disputes, feeling it to be her responsibility to wield her power on behalf of her daughter. For example, she explained how a teacher had taken a particular dislike to Amy and was treating her unfairly:

But going back to when she first went to school [laughs], she had this teacher, Mrs Bell, who actually is not that old but has got this Lee Remick haircut [laughs]. She keeps herself all so well made up. Her lipstick is never out of place. I feel very sorry for her 'cos her daughter actually died in a car crash . . . But having said that, she particularly didn't like Amy . . . so about a week or two later there was a couple of dyslexic twins in her class. And she made friends with them. And then once she'd been there a week or two later AND SHE SHOULD HAVE KNOWN THE RULES BY NOW, according to the teacher, and she painted them . . . [laughs]. Their brand new school uniforms were painted [laughs]. But according to Amy. And I'm inclined to believe Amy's version that they all decided that they were going to go in and do painting and started splashing paint. But Amy got the blame for it. . . . And basically it like came out that because Amy wouldn't like settle, the teacher used to sit her off the carpet and on to the floor. But instead of each time, doing it each time when it came to story time. Each time Amy sort of like mucked about a bit, she would do it every time. So whenever it went to story time she'd say, 'Right, Amy, you sit over there', on this cold floor, whilst all the kids sat on the floor for story time. So I actually wrote her a letter and I said not only was it

> unfair to Amy and she's actually getting cold. 'Cos she'd then began to complain about it 'cos she knew that we weren't approving of it. And I said it's also a lazy form of teaching. And I said I do understand that Amy is hyperactive and she finds it difficult to settle, but she will never settle if you never give her the chance to. And I said I want to find her back with the other group of children.

It is notable that Nina's disputes are conducted at a highly personal level. By isolating particular individuals within institutions, she establishes her battlegrounds and identifies the targets to be fought against. As with the 'venomous' housing assistant, Mrs Bell represents an important focus for Nina's anger and frustration at the way she and her daughter are consistently wronged, scapegoated or ignored by such organisations. As this extract demonstrates, Nina effectively defuses the potential threat of Mrs Bell by mocking her and discrediting her actions as a teacher. First Nina challenges Mrs Bell's authority through ridiculing her appearance, drawing attention to her 'Lee Remick haircut' and her make up. Even Nina's acknowledgement that she feels sorry for Mrs Bell because her daughter died in a car crash serves to reinforce an image of a sad but rather comical character. Nina's laughter as she relayed this description further emphasises her portrayal of the teacher as more absurd than authoritative. The middle classes are often mocked and ridiculed by working-class people (Skeggs 1997, 2006), and Nina demonstrates the powerful psychological effect this can have in undermining status and authority.

Once again, the moral grounds for this dispute are made clear. Mrs Bell had displayed an unreasonable dislike of Amy, unjustly singled her out and blamed her for a joint incident of misbehaviour. This discrimination is then described as carrying over into routine school activities, resulting in Amy's unfair isolation on the cold floor on the unjustifiable basis that she might otherwise play up. Mrs Bell is presented as acting immorally both by discriminating against Amy and teaching unprofessionally. Nina's demand for Amy to be included with the other children is presented as an order, thereby challenging the teacher's authority and asserting her own. Nina's distinctly antagonistic approach to dealing with formal institutions was not typical of the other mothers in my research, although she may share commonalities with the many working-class parents who are labelled as aggressive or unreasonable by professionals. Nevertheless, many of the mothers found themselves driven to extreme measures, such as condoning truancy or harassing a teacher, in order to protect or defend their children. Such battles were always underpinned by a moral claim upon which arguments were sustained or conceded. For example, Carol, a white working-class mother described how she had twice defended her son 'to the realms' only to discover that he had indeed flashed his bum in the playground and broken a window. On finding out she was wrong, Carol paid for the damage and reflected that the teacher had after all been reasonable.

For the middle-class parents in the *Resources in Parenting* study, disputes with teachers were generally played out through a very different power dynamic. Although they were just as concerned to ensure justice for their children, they rarely found themselves in direct conflict with teachers. Significant cultural and social capital could usually be mobilised in order to quietly and efficiently negotiate problems with teachers or children. Many middle-class parents monitored classroom activities, keeping a close eye on their children and their teachers. Many also involved themselves with PTAs or stood as school governors. Where disputes did arise, such parents could usually command significant respect and power. A resolute belief in their child's deserved high status within the school was a significant feature shaping interactions with teachers, as Jennifer, a white middle-class mother from the *Resources in Parenting* study, illustrates:

> It [complaint about the teacher] did happen with Chloe and an English teacher, last year, which was unusual with Chloe because she is bright and popular, teachers like her, so after a while I started writing down the things she said . . . then I went to the parents evening, I did speak to him about it but he really didn't like it, I said 'She says you don't like her', and er . . . that sort of thing but he really took offence, but after that he was, he said to her . . . I don't know why you told your mum I don't like you, sort of thing, but after that he was better about that, it was sort of dealt with . . . sometimes if they know that you're aware of it that's all it needs really.

Class and race and schooling

Two out of the four non-white working-class mothers in this research were engaged in particularly bitter disputes with their children's schools. Examining these examples in detail provides some insight into the way institutional racism both compounds and is compounded by class disadvantage. Although these experiences are discussed solely from the viewpoint of the mothers concerned, they are contextualised by national statistics revealing the sustained and disproportionate educational disadvantage suffered by many ethnic minority pupils (DfES 2005). Just as the current trend to blame parents for children's attainment and behaviour in the classroom does not acknowledge the classed nature of childrearing, the impact of racism is also similarly overlooked. Yet numerous studies demonstrate how schools are founded on practices that reproduce racial as well as class privilege (van Dijk 1993; Cole 2004). As Deborah Youdell's (2003, 2004) research effectively demonstrates, these practices circulate at multiple levels through the education system, from bureaucratic policy-making to everyday interactions in the classroom. In her study of Caribbean mothers in the UK, Tracey Reynolds (2005) shows how a central part of being a black mother involves developing strategies to enable children to cope with racism.

A case study focus on Julie (also discussed in Chapter 4) reveals the particular challenges that working-class, black mothers negotiate in relation to their children's school. Julie, an African-Caribbean lone mother of two (Lloyd 15 and Carly 10) explained how she had only been dating Lloyd's father for two weeks before she fell pregnant. The relationship did not last very long and after Lloyd was born, Julie became involved with another man. This relationship lasted three years, during which time Julie had several miscarriages. Although Carly was not explicitly planned, Julie had hoped her birth might help bring her closer to Carly's father. However, they eventually split up and Julie found herself parenting alone and dependent on welfare benefits. The children see their fathers very occasionally, but Julie has a tight network of friends and family that help her to get by on a day-to-day basis (see Chapter 4).

Carly is currently at an ethnically mixed primary school, but Lloyd attends Griffindale, a predominantly white secondary school. While Griffindale school is below national averages in terms of performance, it is viewed as considerably better than the other main school in the area, Grangers, which has a high ethnic minority intake. Grangers has a very poor reputation and low pupil attainment. Despite the clear differences in quality between the two schools, Julie does not feel that Lloyd has benefited from attending Griffindale. His marks have been consistently low and he is regularly in trouble over his behaviour. Julie is extremely distressed by this and has been in contact with the school in an attempt to remedy the situation. She feels strongly that Lloyd is the victim of racial discrimination by teachers, but has been unable to get the school to recognise this. Julie has at times been overwhelmed by the extent of unfair treatment she sees meted out to Lloyd and has fought hard against particular accusations levelled against him. After years of challenging this injustice she now feels that Lloyd will be better off leaving the school:

I feel that the school system let me down . . . there was loads of fabrications, allegations, you know, and like the school system let me down and to be honest the sooner he finishes from that school, you know, the better it will be for me. Because, I mean, they just told loads of lies, you know, they've targeted my son for whatever reasons, well I know discrimination, yeah, because like the school is like, erm, don't get me wrong, it's, erm, very very very high standard of education, yeah, very very high standard of education and, erm, it's predominantly, erm, a Caucasian school, I just use that word for want of a better word, Caucasian and, you know, there's been, and I feel that his, not to say that I'm just not quite, er, in coming to me own decision, you know, I've heard from word of mouth, you know, when it comes to like black children, they get like the raw end of the stick, you know. Yeah, yeah, so, you know, because, you know, and even like, erm, certain incidents, I mean, I've had to like go to the Citizens Advice, I've had to phone the Education Committee you know, just to get help because like there's these situations where I feel like Lloyd's wrongly, you know.

Julie eventually reached a point of exhaustion in her dispute with the school, and this fatigue was compounded by several family bereavements. Particularly devastating was the suicide of one of her sisters, which left her feeling unable to cope for a while. She expressed strong anger that the school cut Lloyd little slack during this dreadful and distressing period for their family. Julie described how she was continually harassed about Lloyd's absent homework, but felt too traumatised to engage properly with the school over it. During this time Lloyd had persuaded a classmate from a top set to help him out by writing an essay which he them submitted as his own. The 'F' mark he subsequently received confirmed to Julie that he was being actively discriminated against. As the following quote demonstrates, Julie is convinced her son is being victimised, but she feels relatively powerless to alter the situation:

She kept on phoning me, saying 'Mrs Denis, it's Lloyd's English teacher here, I'm just phoning to say like Lloyd's not brought his homework in and every time he doesn't bring his homework in he's gonna stay for detention, and every time he doesn't stay for detention, he's gonna do lines,' you know, and the thing is that the teacher knew because, like, Lloyd's been off for like a long length of time, you know, going through like the grieving period and that. And, like, there was one time when, like, this is like the day after and then she phoned once again, she goes, 'Mrs Denis, it's Lloyd's teacher here, I'm gonna have to leave Lloyd behind in school because he's not bringing in, you know, his homework.' And I was really pissed off because like the work that he produced, you know, it was fantastic and I thought I needed to go round and see this one, but because I was going through the motions I wanted to, like, to help me son but because I was like going through the grieving period, nothing matters, but I mean nothing mattered so I couldn't go down and like deal with it but I felt at the time it was unfair and unjust and the school system let me down because they knew what I was going through and then this teacher here, this young English teacher, she had no right like playing with me son's education.

Having given up on the school, Julie is pinning her hopes on Lloyd getting a second chance at education by gaining a place in an further education (FE) college. Research by Hedi Mirza (1995) suggests that black women often rely on the 'backdoor route' of FE to gain the education qualifications they were unable to secure at school. Although she has no qualifications herself and has had a demoralising experience of school both as a pupil and parent, Julie still attaches great significance to education. Carly is nearing her secondary transfer age and Julie will shortly have to decide which school to send her to. She faces a painful dilemma: she is forced to choose between exposing her daughter to the racist practices of Griffendale or the educationally sub-standard Grangers school. Despite her recriminations, Julie feels it is still probably in her daughter's best interests to attend Griffendale. She hopes Carly will be more successful in fitting in at the school than Lloyd. As Patricia Hill Collins (1994) notes, black mothers are often faced with difficult decisions about whether to encourage their children to assimilate or to confront racism head-on.

As I outlined in Chapter 2, issues of class and race/ethnicity are intimately intertwined. In her study of Caribbean mothers in the UK, Tracey Reynolds (2005) found her middle-class interviewees had more positive experiences of education than their working-class counterparts. She speculated that teachers may find more affinity with middle-class as opposed to working-class black children. This is supported by Deborah Youdell's (2004) classroom ethnography, which suggests teachers evaluate pupils against a template of an individualised, white, middle-class 'ideal learner'. Those falling short might be viewed as 'treatable', while 'others' become inscribed as 'hopeless'. This research also highlights the subtle but powerful nature of more middle-class forms of racism, as opposed to the overt and conscious discrimination it has become associated with. Like most black people, Julie has had experience of both forms of racism, but feels more able to deal with the direct and easily identifiable kind. She described how Carly's school responded promptly in the context of explicit racial abuse:

> There was this other incident where, like, this boy kept on saying [to Carly], erm, 'You're a blackie you're a nigger.' . . . So, erm, I looked at the little boy and I said 'We're going to the teacher about you.' . . . So anyway, I went to see the teacher and to cut a long story short, you know, she said she didn't realise, you know, that Carly, you know, this boy was, you know, like, behaving that way towards Carly. So she brought it to the attention of, like, the headmaster. . . . When Carly started it was predominantly a Caucasian school, yeah, and apparently what happened, because of the upbringing of the little boy, he didn't, he didn't know any better, you know, he's never been in contact with, like, black people, believe it or not. So what happened, like erm, the headmaster got them to do in assembley on Friday, you know, to talk, well to act out, you know, what it's like, like different, you know, like, cultures, like to get together so that's how they dealt with it, which I thought was, like, fantastic, you know.

Despite the distressing nature of this incident, Julie expresses considerable tolerance and understanding. The racism described here is unambiguous and easily challenged, and while the hurt cannot be undone, Julie is reassured by the school's recognition of this wrong. This is something she is unable to obtain in the context of her son. In the institutional arena of the school, racism circulates in a less obvious but arguably more devastating fashion, and Julie finds herself relatively powerless in her efforts to confront it. Teachers are rarely keen to acknowledge the significance of race in their classrooms and often claim to adopt a 'colour-blind' approach (Reynolds 2005). As a black working-class mother, Julie commands little authority and is vulnerable to being ignored or discredited. She is well aware of the low status accorded to her by teachers and is reflexive and strategic in attempting to pre-empt likely racist misinterpretations. For example, she considers what she would do if another problem were to arise with the school:

> I'd want to know and just take it from there. . . . But not go off me head or, you know, obviously be rational because that's what, that's what they would love, you know, you know, once again, you know, lots

of things are stereotyped, you know, as far as, like, when it come to ethnic parents, you know, they're just like [pause] in the face of the, you know, you don't come across very diplomatic, you know. No, I'd go down and be very very diplomatic, you know, and just sort it out really.

Julie was not the only ethnic minority mother in this study to consciously consider tactics in dealing with institutional racism. Meena (the Indian mother discussed in Chapter 3) was involved in a long-running dispute with her eldest sons' school. Both boys were consistently subjected to violence and harassment from white boys at their school. They are regularly beaten up on their way to and from school, abused and have had their Nike baseball caps stolen from them. The boys fight back but then often find themselves in trouble with the teachers. Meena feels her complaints to the school are largely ignored, while she is repeatedly called in to account for her own boys' bad behaviour in the classroom. In the case of the baseball caps, which were snatched in the playground, one was returned after a complaint to the head. Meena is furious that the school is not concerned enough to retrieve the other. She is also angry that incidents of abuse and bullying go unpunished, even where there are adult witnesses:

One time my friend said to me, 'Do you know that yesterday that boy was beating your Raj?' so I said 'No'. So when I asked my son 'Why didn't you tell me that yesterday that boy was trying to beat you?', he said 'How you know mum?' so I said 'My friend who lives in front of the school, she told me'. Jane's mum, my small son's class one girl he study with, 'Jane's mum told me', 'Yes mum, I forgot to tell you'. Because kids don't want to tell everything to mum because, you know. So then I tell to the teacher again, the class teacher 'that yesterday that boy was trying to beat my son, Jane's mum told me', so witness are her. Nothing happened, nothing happens, no response. No good response . . . we know, we tell the teacher, this is the boy's name, I think it was Jo, one was Jo he's in my son's class. If anything happens with my son, nobody takes any good response. But if my son do anything to other boy, straight away the teacher 'Oh, your son did this', so it's not good for us. We don't want to be [inaudible] my son hits somebody else or, we don't want like this even our self. I can understand if it is my son fault, I will tell him not to do this again strictly, but if anything happens with my son it's not good even . . .

Is it always the same children?

Yes, mostly. Then I was going to school and pick them up so I've been early, so I was standing before they came out. So one son was trying to just, he was trying to hit him, so I said 'What's going on?' from the back, so he said 'He's doing this', so I said 'You can't touch him, if he's doing anything tell your class teacher'. The boy said in front of me 'Yes, I can touch your son' and he just banged to his shoulder like this 'Yes, I can touch your son' and I said to him 'You can't touch my son like this, you can't hit him, if you have any problem with him tell your class teacher and she will sort it out', so he said 'Yes I can touch your son'.

Meena did not speak explicitly in terms of racism, possibly because she did not feel comfortable discussing this with a white researcher. However, her struggles are clearly racialised and have much in common with other Asian families in the community. Many of Meena's friends have had similar experiences, with one having felt compelled to take her daughter out of the school. Meena and her husband are considering a similar move but there are no alternative schools nearby. The children have to be accompanied to and from school for their own safety, and longer journeys would be impossible to fit into the family's already gruelling schedule (see Chapter 3). Like Julie, Meena tries to stay calm and pursue strategies that are sanctioned by white middle-class institutions. For example, Meena and a number of Asian mothers got together to write a letter to the education department detailing their grievances. This took time and effort, particularly given that English is a second language for the women. Several months have past and no reply has yet been received. Like Julie, Meena is left with a strong sense of injustice, but little power to fight it:

Yes, this is our life, this is our world. I want to be safe place for my kids. Safe school, the teacher can understand parents, whether it is Indian or whether it is English or whether it is any other culture. Because children are going to school if they have any problems it should be sorted out.

The examples of Julie and Meena demonstrate the difficulties in attempting to separate out issues of race and class. Clearly ethnic minority middle-class families are also subjected to racism, but their experiences are likely to be very different. Their cultural capital affords them greater status and 'knowledge', they can often count on influential friends and social contacts to back them up, and their financial situation usually ensures that they avoid the catchment areas of the most 'troubled' schools. Access to these capitals may not always be enough to counter the impact of racism but they undoubtedly offer much greater protection.

In the *Resources in Parenting* study, a middle-class Ugandan Asian mother described her daughter's problems fitting in at her private school and disputes with the teachers about the standard of her work. Using a similar technique to Katherine (the white, middle-class mother described in the previous chapter), she drew on her financial advantage and obtained a specialist report confirming her daughter was 'gifted and talented'. Being middle class can mean black mothers are able to claim a deservingness that represents a powerful challenge to racism. For working-class mothers who are black, racist practices are often remain hidden beneath naturalised, class-coded distinctions.

Conclusion: marginalised perspectives on institutional spaces

My focus in this chapter has been how encounters with formal organisations and professionals are actually experienced and interpreted by working-class mothers. The examples I've outlined so far highlight the gap between institutional values and expectations, and the day-to-day lives of the mothers. Teachers, health visitors, housing officers and other professionals often have limited understanding of the circumstances framing the behaviour and reasoning of their clients, and have even less time to explore this as a meaningful context (Gillies 2006b). Principles and values underpinning institutions tend to be grounded in middle-class privilege, yet conveyed as self-evident truths. For example, 'good' mothers are expected to ensure cultural consistency between home and school. Working class mothers who maintain protective boundaries between these two arenas are then perceived not to care about their children's education and future.

As Annette Lareau notes, 'Educators can adopt relatively rigid definitions of what constitutes helpful behaviour [from parents]; actions that fall outside those bounds are ignored and discredited' (2003: 196). Parents like Nina who harbour a strong sense of injustice are likely to be condemned as unreasonable and aggressive. Her grievances cannot be understood from a standpoint that assumes fairness and respect is equally accessible. Similarly, the institutional racism experienced by Julie and Meena is embedded within ideals of individualistic meritocracy. Standards that resonate with and benefit the white middle classes tend to do so at the expense of those they make 'other'. Yet an illusion of justice is sustained through the moral judgements attached to particular behaviours of children and parents. This imposition of middle-class values on working-class lives inevitably pathologises, but, as the next chapter demonstrates, it also prioritises regulation over support.

Chapter 6

Working-class mothering
Strengths and values

So far this book has explored working-class mothers' accounts of their lives, highlighting the way meanings are grounded in particular social and material realities. In this chapter the focus is on the way these situated understandings allow the mothers to generate crucial resources for their children. I begin by considering the status and significance these women attach to motherhood. In spite of unremittingly negative public portrayals of 'pram-faces' and chavettes, most of the women in my research forged an extremely positive identity around mothering, emphasising satisfaction, pleasure and competence. In a context of deprivation and struggle, being a mother was valued and prioritised and was characterised by resilience and determination. The significance of home for the mothers in the study is further underlined in this chapter through a focus on the emotional resources made available to children. I show how crucial (though easily overlooked) home-based efforts to repair children's self-esteem, protect them from harm and promote their educational and future prospects can be viewed in terms of 'emotional capital'. These emotional investments ensure mothering practices are tailored to reflect the specific challenges faced by working-class families on a day-to-day basis.

Becoming a mum

> Like it's an important part that now I am like mum, I become a mum, from girl. I become first a lady and after the lady I become mum. It's quite a good change, isn't it?
>
> (Meena – Indian working-class mother)

Motherhood entails change in identity for all women. For the mothers in this research it was the source of great pride and self-respect, with many discussing how having a child marked an important point of transition to adulthood. Several of the mothers were very young when they first became pregnant, but for most their first child was experienced as introducing new depth and meaning to life. Despite prominent negative public portrayals of young motherhood, qualitative research has revealed the way such mothers create their own positive meanings around becoming a parent (Kirkman *et al.* 2001; Proweller 2000; Fine and Weis 1998). The example of Sam, the white, working-class lone mother discussed in Chapter 3, illustrates the way young motherhood can be experienced as a positive new start in life, enabling powerful self-development. Sam had desperately wanted a baby and invested in a heterosexual relationship with Kevin soon after leaving school. She described feelings of euphoria when pushing her first child's pram through the park, noting how often people would stop and remark on how beautiful her daughter was:

> She was, like, the first grandchild on each side . . . And he [Kevin] absolutely idolised her. Everybody did, you used to take her out on the street and people used to look and stare at her, 'cos she was so beautiful . . . Yeah, like, she's very, very, um. She's special. I don't know. She, 'cos because she, she brought out a hell of a lot of love in people. People could look at her and say, oh she's lovely. She brought out a hell of a lot of love out of people and being the first grandchild as well.

While Sam's relationship with Kevin was characterised by abuse and hardship (see Chapter 3), there is no regret associated with her decision to have children with him. A new life began for Sam once she was finally able to gain independence as a lone mother. Her proven ability to bring two children up with little support from their father is clearly the source of great pride and satisfaction for her. Being a single mother is depicted as difficult and challenging but ultimately very rewarding, providing a number of advantages above dual parenting. In her account Sam describes the process of mothering as a 'job', requiring skill, ability and devotion. Coping alone intensifies the need for competence and efficiency, but it also increases the fulfilment that can be gained from parenting.

Sam's account of becoming a single mother was told as a story of progress and achievement, and was linked to her personal development as an individual. She explained how her decision to give up on Kevin and parent alone marked a powerful subjective change in her, forcing her to become more independent and assertive. A personality change from being, in her words, 'as soft as shit' to become fiercely self-reliant and confident is interpreted as a direct consequence of becoming a mother. According to Sam, commitment to her children led her to become more ruthless in securing what she identified as their interdependent needs. She accepts sole responsibility for her children, and this requires strength and determination. Realisation that she possesses such traits, combined with mounting evidence of her ability to cope alone, resulted in a dramatically altered self-perception.

This narrative of self-development, from 'young minded' emotional dependency to capable self-determination, constitutes Sam's experience of becoming a single mother. The process of coping alone is presented as self-evidently worthy and indicative of strength of character. Consequently, Sam appropriates the term 'single mother' to construct a positive self-identity as a proficient, independent and responsible individual. Sam is able to articulate this construction despite alternative public representations of single mothers as weak, unable to control their children, and dependent on the state. Her lack of engagement with these negative portrayals underlines the powerful status she attaches to single motherhood. Rather than perceiving her experiences in terms of failure, an assumption commonly superimposed onto the lives of working-class lone parents, Sam emphasises her success in achieving the status of being a single mother.

The significance Sam attaches to being a lone mother and the satisfaction and self-worth she derives from this status is further emphasised by her determination to remain a lone parent. From Sam's perspective, she and the children have too much to lose by returning to the vulnerability of two-parent relationships. As well as stressing her contentment with her current family arrangement, she discussed the advantages of parenting alone, making it clear that she had no intention of risking her independence and control by allowing another man to live with herself and her children. She explained how their negative experience with Kevin had dented her trust and made her aware of the practical and emotional dangers of 'getting serious' with another man. She expressed particular resentment at the way Kevin's actions had impacted on her achievements, ruining her attempts to build a home:

> Because of what happened in Birchwood, like, I had my own home there and I was really trying hard to build it up. And because I've built it up, this, as my own home, and no one's done it except for me. And I've bought everything, he hasn't done anything. . . . And thing is, it's like my home, you know.

Having to move from the house in Birchwood after putting time, attention and money into 'building it up' was experienced as frustrating and disempowering for Sam. Although Kevin was eventually evicted, his perceived stake in the house and the family forced Sam to give up and start all over again. While she described how upsetting this was, she also explained how it provided her with scope to 'build' a stronger, self-contained environment. Sam drew on this metaphor of 'building' often when discussing her role as a mother. For example, she spoke of building her children's confidence, building their lives together as well as building a 'home'. This identification as an architect of her own and her children's future is significant, revealing her sense of responsibility to create opportunities and resources for her children to draw on. While many of the other mothers in the sample associated financial and practical support with the role of a father, Sam accepted and valued this responsibility as a requirement of lone motherhood. Although she described Kevin as a 'good father' for making financial contributions to the children's upbringing, her own efforts in bringing in and managing money are emphasised.

In accepting responsibility for providing resources and 'building' opportunities for her children, Sam fulfils what she perceives to be the duties of motherhood and increases her experience of autonomy and self-sufficiency. As the previous quote demonstrates, she placed great stress on the personal satisfaction she gains from accomplishing things by herself. Her description of her home as an achievement that she constructed conveys the powerful sense of pleasure she derives from successfully completing tasks by herself. Allowing another man to take a share in these tasks is seen by Sam as risky, and she is anxious to maintain a secure boundary around what she perceived as belonging to herself and her children:

> 'Cos I like being a single mum, I don't like people interfering, like, with what I do. Even Kevin, if he says anything to me about the kids, it gets on my nerves and I think to myself, I'm doing my bloody best here and I know I'm doing a really good job. . . . If he did say I used to have to take notice, but now I don't 'cos I don't have to. I don't need to. He's married, he's got his own and I've got my own.

Perhaps not surprisingly, men were regarded as the major threat by Sam to her reconstructed life with her children. She explained how boyfriends are kept away from the house and from the children, out of fear that they may get too involved and 'spoil' what she has achieved. The insecurity that Sam clearly experiences exposes the fragility in her sense of control and confidence. While she feels satisfied and proud of her efforts as a mother, she is acutely aware of her position as vulnerable, and of the need to protect what she has accomplished against the odds. While Sam's fierce determination to parent alone was not shared by other mother's in the research, her dedication and resilience was evident across the sample. The working-class mothers in this book prioritised the needs of their children often at great personal expense.

Mediating the effects of trauma and impoverishment

Like Sam, many of the mothers coped with violence, homelessness and hardship as part of their efforts to nurture, protect and care for their children. These mothers could not conceive of their lives without their children. Moving on without them (as many fathers had done) was simply not a thinkable option. This unspoken but iron commitment sustained them through danger and deprivation, and many felt proud of their ability to parent well in these highly demanding circumstances. But, as the example of Kelly demonstrates, this struggle for survival can be precarious and costly for parents and their children.

Kelly is a white, working-class mother who lives with her two children, Craig (aged 9), Rosie (aged 7), her new partner Terry and his daughter, Jade (aged 7), from a previous relationship. The family live in a rented house in a small town and Terry works as a lorry driver. Kelly had Craig when she was 19 and had always wanted children. Although several of her friends had babies from 14 onwards, she had thought it best to wait until she was a bit older. Her relationship with the children's father, Dean, was not particularly happy, but the family lived together in a small flat and Rosie was born two years later. Dean was not working by this time, and was becoming increasingly violent and abusive. Eventually, fearing for the children's safety, Kelly fled to a women's refuge.

This was a particularly difficult and distressing period for Kelly and the children. Social services became involved and it was discovered that both children had been severely sexually abused. The police were not able to establish who the culprit was, although Dean remains a strong suspect. During this time Kelly and the children lived in fear and grinding poverty (see Chapter 2). They were forced to relocate to different parts of the country several times, which involved packing up and moving home at short notice. The family struggled to survive on benefits, and Kelly often went without food to make sure the children had enough to eat.

Eventually they were able to settle, and Kelly's mother and sister moved from the other side of the country to live nearby. Kelly met Terry shortly after and they decided to rent a house and move in together. However, by then Craig's behaviour had become a focus of concern. He has been diagnosed with conduct disorder and his behaviour is often dangerous and out of control. He starts fires, fights, steals and stays out all night. Although for the last few years he has attended appointments with a psychologist from the local Child and Family Consultation Service, his behaviour appears to be getting worse. Teachers at his school will now only allow him to attend mornings because he is so disruptive. Kelly describes a catalogue of incidents, and focuses on the week before the interview as an example:

Tuesday morning I was in here and we've got garages across there at the back and I stood at that window and I looked out and all I see was the back of him in flames at the front. So I went running out there because I wasn't sure whether he was on fire or whether he'd set fire to something he was holding. And what he'd done is, he'd took a lighter and took a hairspray can and was setting fire to the hairspray can, setting fire to the hairspray can in the air. That was on the Tuesday and so I went into the school and said to them, look, please just keep him in all day. They said 'Yeah, all right, we'll try and keep him in'. Then on the Thursday he'd come home and he'd bought a [toy] gun from a shop out of all the money that he'd took out of my car. And I've had no guns, no toy knives, and that's been a rule since they was babies. So they know they're not allowed. So I took it off him on the Thursday and he actually hit me and smashed his room up to the extent that there was no furniture that was actually savable. He had no bed or nothing left.

Kelly is exhausted and overwhelmed, but gets little sympathy or support from Terry who has washed his hands of Craig. From Terry's perspective Craig is 'a little git, end of story'. Terry works long hours and is often away from home, and to avoid arguments the couple have agreed not to talk about Craig. Kelly has had lots of professional intervention over the years from social services, Child and Adolescent Mental Health workers, parenting advisors, the NSPCC, as well as the police and fire brigade. However, with the exception of the emergency services, the support offered has been confined to counselling, advice or therapy with very little practical help. After discovering the sexual abuse, social services were able to offer a counselling referral for both children, yet were not able ensure the family had a safe, decent and permanent house to live in. When Craig's behaviour problems emerged, Kelly struggled to access meaningful help and found herself pushed towards inappropriate services such as parenting classes:

I've been to the parent group, which is supposed to tell you how to deal with it and that and um that was crap [laughs]. Basically, the ideas were good if I had a 4- or 5-year-old, but for him things like spending 10 minutes on the chair were supposed to calm him down if he was throwing a tantrum. I if I put him on the chair for 10 minutes he'd just laugh, get up and do what ever he was doing before. I didn't find that very helpful at all. I find that going to the authorities and that just hasn't helped at all. I mean, they give me this silly parent book thing and it was just a waste of time. I mean, eight weeks I was going there and we got nothing out of it at all . . . they'd say to me things like 'make sure you do 10 minutes a day playing with him'. Well I've always spent time with my kids anyway, so that really didn't make a difference and I'd say to them, right, because Craig is so severe I sometimes send him to his room for the whole night. So how do I do that 10-minutes' playing with him if I've sent him to his room for being naughty? So that just didn't make sense and they'd say, well, you shouldn't be sending him to his room all night. And my argument was, 10-minutes' punishment is just not enough for Craig. Ten minutes is nothing, like he'll just sit there and go into a daydream and get up and just be the same as he was.

Referring Kelly to parenting classes ignores the wider context shaping Craig's conduct. While his disturbed behaviour is most likely rooted in the violence and upheaval shaping his formative years, it is Kelly's parenting abilities that are questioned, as opposed to the state's failure to protect a vulnerable young mother and her children. Despite the severity of the problem, Kelly has received relatively little useful support from professionals and feels she has been let down. The strain of caring for Craig is immense and she is grateful for any help she can get. Craig's school have now decided to apply for him to attend a specialist residential facility and Kelly is hopeful that this will provide both her and the teachers with a much needed break. She described how the worry often overwhelmed her and made her ill:

I'm not too bad at the moment, but his behaviour has got to the extent where his behaviour has affected my health, and I've ended up at the hospital all night and getting ECG's and things. But it's been panic attacks I've been having and there's been times where I've just had to stop my car when I've been driving, where things have just got on top of me and I've burst out it tears and that. But luckily I've got, like, my mum supports me, if she sees it's getting too much she'll take him for me for a couple of days. But I can go two or three nights where I just deal with it and just cope with it. Just get on with it.

Kelly is able to access crucial support from her mother and her sister, who both live nearby, but these relationships are highly reciprocal and often demanding in their own right. Kelly's mother and sister are both coping with serious problems of their own which Kelly also has to deal with. Although she often turns to her family, she is keen not to overburden them:

> I don't really ask her [sister] for support in a lot of things. I mean she will like, if I say to her like I need the kids picking up from school, she will pick them up. I don't tend to ask her very often. I tend to try and do it all on my own, but I did I mean I did have a fairly bad day. I had a breakdown, I'd left the school and 9.15 and broke down in my car crying and I phoned her up and said get rid of your other half I need to come round for a whinge. And she sent him out to do some stuff and that and I got there in floods of tears and she was like 'what happened?' I just had a scare where I though Craig was on drugs, but he weren't. And sort of we sat and talked about it. And my mum was having quite a few problems of her own at the time, so I didn't really want to go to her. So if Tina [sister] wasn't about I wouldn't have gone to anyone. But she is there, if I need emotional support she is there. And if she needs emotional support she comes to me. And I do find sometimes when I'm sitting here thinking and all my own problems are going through my head, and then my sister's and then my mum's, and sort of my head just feels like it's going to explode by the end of the day.

Links are often made between juvenile delinquency and poor parenting (see Gillies 2000), but the example of Kelly highlights the less visible but central role mothers often play in terms of preventing problems from escalating and continuing to care for children in desperate circumstances. The consistently grim prospects for children looked after by local authorities bears testament to the significance of this role, with care leavers considerably more likely to end up homeless, using drugs and or in prison (Ward *et al.* 2003; Robbins 2001; Utting 1997). Far from suggesting any parenting deficit, Kelly's account reveals the extent of energy she devotes to mothering her three children. Also prominent is the pleasure and satisfaction she continues to derive from parenting, alongside the pain and worry. Despite the difficulties with Craig, Kelly clearly feels she is a good mother and she emphasises her skills in looking after children. When her daughter joined a local children's club (Badgers), Kelly became involved as a parent helper and proudly describes herself as among the most qualified, longstanding helpers in the district. In short, Kelly gains great happiness for caring from children, and her life revolves around her own children:

> I don't really get much time to myself because Craig, like today he does 9 till half past 12 at school and I've got him here all afternoon. Then in the evening I've got him here. Then other days he don't got to school till quarter past one and he comes home at 3, which doesn't give you a lot of time to go out, even to do shopping or anything. It's just hard work just getting little jobs done. . . . Yeah, so the only time I really get to my self is when I'm asleep.
>
> Do you think it's important for you to have time on your own?
>
> Not really, 'cos I do like doing a lot of stuff with kids and that anyway, I can sort of get down to their level and play their games and I sort out craft ideas and things for Badgers, and I always get my lot to try it all out before hand anyway. So we do a lot of making things and try new games together, and it's not too bad then.
>
> If you manage to get time on your own, how do you spend it?
>
> Well, I don't really do time on me own. Because if there's no kids around about I'll go round and play with my sister's little boy who's coming up to 2. Or I'll go round and see if my mum's alright, because she's not been very well. So I don't really do time by on my own, I think I'd be quite – what do I do with myself if I did have time to myself? . . . Probably get a job.
>
> Mmh, what would you like to do?
>
> Work in a nursery [laughs].

The limited period that Craig spends at school is compounding his severely restricted educational development. Kelly expressed particular shock and disappointment that teachers have not been able to provide him with basic reading skills. He is not receiving any special/professional help at school or at home and Kelly is resigned to the prospect of relying on her own efforts to teach him. However, Kelly struggles herself to understand the work that Craig brings home and has instead bought some basic textbooks to go through with him:

I just don't understand how the school have let his reading age slip so low. Then they're giving him written instructions that they know he can't read, and then he gets told off and sent home because he's . . . Instead of him saying, look, I can't do it, he'll misbehave, but they've got the special needs report there saying he's got a reading age of 4.6 and he's sort of nearly 10 years old and they're giving him stuff that normal 10-year-olds should be able to read. 'Cos they said he needs to learn the basics and that as well, and I'm aware that they haven't got the facilities there to do it. They've got all them kids there that they've got to teach, they can't devote the time to one. So I've said that I'm quite happy to have him at home and when he's at home we've got books that we do and we've got the learning one for the computer that he does as well and so, it's picking him up a little bit. I'm doing the basic English and taking him back to step 1 really and doing that with him at the moment. So I don't really get involved with what he's doing at school because he's in so much trouble at school. Sort of school stays at school and I do our bits at home. I've got some special books and things that I've bought and we do them rather than doing what ever he's doing at school.

The example of Kelly highlights the way working-class families are disadvantaged by dominant discourses which construct parents as responsible for their children's learning. While middle-class parents can draw on their own knowledge, cultural values, social contacts and financial resources to support their children's educational development, working-class parents are forced to depend more heavily on teachers. As I outlined in Chapter 4, working-class parents have a limited sense of entitlement, as Kelly's comment 'they've got all them kids there to teach and they can't devote the time to one' demonstrates. In the context of scarce resources, social stigma and little power or authority, Kelly externalises school failure and devotes her time to helping Craig learn at home.

Like the other mothers in this study, Kelly works hard to compensate for the vulnerability and a lack of access to material and economic resources, but this necessitates a prioritisation of particular principles and practices. Kelly's emphasis on home over school is likely to be misinterpreted as a rejection of education as a value because her behaviour does not conform to ideal models of parental involvement. A fundamental concern with ensuring that children are equipped to deal with instability, injustice and hardship often clashes with more normative middle-class expectations. This is reflected in the different kinds of emotional resources that working-class mothers make available to their children in comparison with middle-class parents.

Valuable feelings: emotions as resources

Despite a general agreement that emotions lay at the heart of family life, this crucial dimension of interpersonal relations is often naturalised to a point of invisibility. Some theorists have attempted to illuminate this complex area by exploring how emotions can act as a family resource, drawing on and widening Bourdieu's model of capitals (Reay 2000, 2002; Allat 1993; Notwotny 1981). This work on 'emotional capital' has been valuable in drawing attention to an under-theorised parenting resource, but has been characterised by a preoccupation with academic attainment. There is a tendency for existing literature on this topic to equate emotional capital with educational success, viewing it as a resource passed on through parental involvement. To count as emotional capital, parental involvement must generate a profit for the child (Reay 2000, 2002). However, this assessment inevitably depends on a value judgement as to what might constitute a 'profit', as is evident in a common conflation between emotional capital as a resource and educational progress as (one particular) outcome (Gillies 2006a).

As I have shown throughout this book, interpretations of the best outcome for children are firmly tied to the material and social positions of their parents. Consequently a more flexible understanding of emotional capital is needed to recognise the value of parental investments without imposing middle-class values on working-class lives. An exploration of the emotions associated with a parent's desire to promote their children's wellbeing and prospects throws light on a range of practices and orientations. This approach allows an appreciation that emotional investments may be directed towards day-to-day survival as well as maximising future opportunities to get ahead. From this perspective emotional capital can be understood as a resource for crucial short-term benefits, as well as more long-term investments in children's futures. This avoids a deficit model of working-class emotional capital by recognising the crucial yet often hidden resources marginalised parents may generate.

At a broad level the emotions of the mothers in this study were aroused to act as a resource in three main contexts: soothing and boosting children's self-esteem, promoting their future interests, and protecting and defending them. While these emotional orientations were generally shared by middle-class mothers in the *Resources in Parenting* study, practices and investments were highly classed. As was discussed in Chapter 4, attainment at school is recognised as having an important impact on children's self-esteem, but while middle-class mothers invested heavily in their child's academic success as a marker of worth, working-class mothers focused on alternative values to mediate the psychological impact of school failure. As I have outlined, middle-class parents can mobilise formidable economic, cultural and social resources to bolster their child's academic success. But while most working-class mothers would love to see their child do well at school, this hope is tempered by a recognition that the odds are stacked against them. Failure is an experience that most working-class children must learn to cope with from an early age. Working class mothers are concerned to ensure that children survive without being emotionally crushed, and this can be played out in strategies such as a disinvestment from school and a prioritisation of home over school (see Gillies 2006a for a more detailed discussion).

Attempts to boost self-esteem are also linked to economic capital in a highly classed way. While a large amount of money might be spent on middle-class children, emotional significance is more often diverted through the values and aspirations associated with middle-class cultural capital. For example, investments might be made in after-school activities, extra tuition, 'educational' toys or computer games, or trips to museums. For working-class mothers, however, giving is more likely to be associated with a notion of worth and deservingness rather than moral or educational appropriateness. Acquiring a high status or much desired item for a child can convey a range of symbolic meanings, heightened by the scarcity of the financial resources that are required to buy it. The following extract from Julie (discussed in Chapter 5) demonstrates the depth of the emotional significance placed on providing something that is desired:

> I've got no money you know, and 'cos I punch me gas and punch me electric it is difficult and also, you know, I've got like, erm, the phone, the phone bill, I've got the [playstation], I've got the [playstation] for the children because they're not ones for asking so I feel well, you know, this is like a reward, you know, like for them. . . . I mean it doesn't bother me whether I get to go on holiday or not, but I do think that, you know, definitely for the children because they don't ask to be brought into this world and because they're here I feel that I need to, you know, give 'em things that they haven't got and because, like, I'm one parent, you know, and yeah, they do see the, like, children out there that's got the best this and the best of that but, you know, I do try and provide.
>
> OK. But what happens if the children really want something but you don't have the money, say like a new pair of trainers or something like that?
>
> By hook or by crook I'll get it. Yeah, by hook or by crook I'll get it and I don't mean, like, going out there and steal it, I just mean, like, just if it means, like, me not paying a bill, I'd just not pay a bill and do it that way.

For Julie, providing things like a playstation or a holiday entails a real struggle that inevitably communicates to her children the extent to which they are valued. For more wealthy parents, spending money is a less obviously significant act and consequently there is likely to be a tension between curbing their children's materialism and making them happy. These parents were much more likely to apply codes and norms in relation to buying things for their children, like helping the child to save for it, or buying it if it is 'needed' for an educational activity. But when money is scarce, treats and gifts are highly meaningful. Much desired items like brand name clothing or a favourite junk food for tea might make a difficult day at school more bearable for a child, while also communicating a strong message of love and care. Yet from a middle-class perspective this might be viewed as an irresponsible extravagance, encouraging consumerism and poor health in a context where money could be better spent.

As is illustrated in Chapter 5, emotions expressed by working-class mothers are often orientated towards the defence of their children and the safeguarding of justice in terms of rights. Emotional capital in this context could be characterised by anger, outrage and burning feelings of injustice, from which children could draw a sense of their own entitlement and a determination to fight back. For parents like Nina and Julie (both discussed in Chapter 5), concern and anger had prompted them to act forcefully in an attempt to protect their children. While both had become embroiled in disputes with teachers, it is likely that their forceful efforts generated tangible benefits for their children. For example, Julie described how she fought hard to clear her son's name when he was accused of assaulting another boy at school:

> If my child's, like, done something, I'd be so humble, yeah, if he'd done something I'd humble myself, yeah? But if I know he's not done anything I'm gonna, like, support him a hundred and ten per cent, yeah? So I'm saying, I went down to the headmaster, you know, to try and like sort this out because it's gone on his record, it's gone in the files, so what the headmaster turned round to me and said, 'Mrs Denis, it's not going to go any further, in fact Lloyd done it but it won't go any further if when he goes to college, whether it be work, you know, it won't be forwarded to his next employer or, you know, college or whatever', so I'm saying well, I don't want it in the filing cabinet because, like, he didn't do it.

Anxiety to ensure children are protected provoked a number of different reactions and strategies by the mothers in the sample. For example, Kelly explained how she besieged a teacher and drew on social contacts to deal with her daughter's vulnerability to bullies:

> I went in every single day and said to her teacher, you know it happened again yesterday. And I done it every single day and I think the teacher just got fed up [laughs]. I've got a friend who's a dinner lady at the school as well and so she watched out for her at dinner time and that as well for me.

For other mothers attention was focused on making sure children are streetwise and able to stand up for themselves. The two African-Caribbean lone mothers in the study were particularly concerned about the vulnerability and confidence of their daughters at school. Julie expressed anxiety that her daughter might be susceptible to people taking advantage of her:

> Carly's just so so so pleasant, you know, you know, she's, erm. Sometimes I do have concerns about Carly's behaviour because, you know, she's so pleasant to the fact that, you know, some people can take advantage of that, you know, with one of [pause] because of her nature. I do try and, like, toughen her up [laughs] because I know what it's like, you know, I know what it's like when you – so I do try to, like, toughen her up.

While Annette expressed her surprise and pride that her daughter was able to challenge the teacher about her grades:

> She's surprised me with being assertive with a couple if the teachers on grades that she's getting. There was one time when she got a 'C' grade for something that she'd done and the week before she got an 'A' grade for something she didn't consider as good, and she actually challenged her teacher, she said 'How is it that I got "A" for that and I spent two hours on this and got a "C" for it?' and the teacher was quite taken aback. She said she felt so proud of herself that she challenged her.

Working-class emotional capital is plentiful in the home with mothers soothing hurt feelings, bolstering confidence and communicating hopes, fears and expectations that are necessarily shaped by social and economic realities. As I have shown, many of the working-class mothers in this study were prepared go into school and passionately defend their children to teachers. But on a day-to-day basis most concentrated on supporting their children outside of this institutional environment. In disputes with other school children, it was common for the mothers to approach other mothers in an effort to resolve the issue without involving teachers.

Educational involvement

While mothers in this sample often prioritised home above school, this does not indicate a lack of interest in children's schooling. Deep concern was expressed about children's future prospects, and the mothers worked hard to ensure their children were not left behind in terms of education. Significantly, though, their strategies were often less visible because they tended to bypass the school system. As I outlined earlier in this chapter, Kelly's emotional investments, by necessity, circumvented the school system, reflecting the choices available to her. She is aware she cannot rely on the school to deal with Craig's disturbed behaviour and low reading age, and she does not have a middle-class voice of authority to demand better provision. Attempts by working-class mothers to address poor resourcing in schools were not well received, as Louise found when she complained about a seemingly endless stream of temporary supply teachers allocated to her daughter's class. She was told she should be grateful the school were providing her daughter with any teachers at all. Notwithstanding the tight funding dilemmas facing many schools, it is difficult to imagine this statement being made to any of the middle-class parents in the *Resources in Parenting* study.

   While the context is very different, the concern, fears and commitments of the working-class mothers in this research are just as valuable and representative of emotional capital as they would be for the parents of academically successful children. Although unlikely to lead to the hard currency of academic qualifications, their efforts represent a highly significant resource in shaping their children's future. Yet the valuable contributions made by working-class mothers in terms of supporting their children's education are rarely recognised because they lack the prominence of more middle-class approaches. For example, from a middle-class professional's point of view, Liz (discussed in Chapter 4) might be questioned in terms of her commitment to her children's education. Like most of the working-class mothers, Liz assumes a largely submissive role with respect to day-to-day school involvement. Contact beyond reports, administrative letters and occasional parents' evenings is rare and associated with being summoned to account for a problem. Yet behind this apparent disinterest there lies considerable anxiety and an everyday labour-intensive struggle to ensure that school work is taken seriously:

> And I do threaten him if he gets a bad school report, which, touch wood, he's not had. But they've got a new scheme now. They're getting three a year at the end of every term. So it's not going to be a year before I know what he's up to. Which I'm pleased because I often wonder, you often wonder how they're getting on really. Because the school doesn't ever contact you, it's hearsay isn't it. He says oh yeah, I'm doing great. But I mean, I do look through his books. Like, I was looking through them last night, and um er, he gets all agitated you know – put them back, put them back – and you know – 'Why are you going through my bag, it's all personal?' You know he doesn't want you to look at anything, and when I ask him things, you know, how he's getting on at school. He's always yeah OK. And he's quite vague about it. . . . I mean, they always say I moan. But I'm not, I don't think I'm moaning all the time, I just will ask him what he's doing. But it's just, in their eyes, it's you're moaning all the time.

While Liz tries to keep herself informed of her oldest son's progress, she relies on limited feedback from him and the teachers. She is grateful for the regular school reports as they tend to provide reassurance that her children are not falling behind or misbehaving. She does not have the sense of entitlement or confidence to ask for more detailed information, and more importantly she would have little use for it. From Liz's perspective a mother's role is to supervise, push and pull her children in the right direction, while education remains the teacher's domain. This is reinforced by a privacy boundary drawn by her son, who views his mother's scrutiny terms of intrusion. Consequently Liz's efforts to support her son's education at home are characterised by 'nagging' and conflict. For example, Liz describes how she feels she has to chide Adam into doing his homework:

> He always has to be pushed though, you know, with the homework. I was moaning at him only last night about he homework. He's one of these boys, you've got to be behind him. If the teacher says well I'd like a small paragraph, then he will write a small paragraph. He'll never think

there's lots more to write about that I'll go and do a whole page. He's like well she wanted a small paragraph and I've done it [laughs], you know . . . You know, and I always say well, there's loads you can write about that. No no, that's all she wanted. And I say well, and it annoys me. . . . And I definitely think that with boys it's just like well, I've done the homework, I'm not going to get a detention now. And I'm moaning at him, you just do the minimum that gets you out of trouble. You know, and I keep saying to him, don't you want to do well at school? He says yeah, I do want to do well at school but I don't want to have to keep doing loads of homework. And I said well, you're not going to get anywhere if you don't put anything in.

Liz admits to 'moaning' and openly acknowledges that Adam's attitude towards his homework annoys her, but she feels a responsibility to keep pushing 'behind him' to ensure he gets the work done. 'Doing the minimum that gets you out of trouble' was identified as a key motive spurring Adam on to do his homework. This resonates with the anxiety Liz expresses about the negative consequences of not following rules (see Chapter 4), but she is clearly frustrated over Adam's reluctance to do the best he can. She plays an active role in persuading, motivating and occasionally pressurising her sons into certain activities for their own good. This responsibility was accepted by Liz as an inevitable feature of mothering, but it was also a source of concern and worry for her:

You know, I think, I think definitely since he's been a teenager I've definitely noticed a lack of, um, he's quite, he's not hard work, but he definitely needs that shove all the time. And um, he is quite happy to lollop about, and TV on, and you run around getting things for him. And unless you, like, you know, he does ask me to get things. And I say, you know, what's wrong with you getting up and getting it? 'Cos I don't want them all the time being waited on hand on foot. Because when they grow older they're going to find things really difficult. And he is quite, um, a lazy boy. And I'm always having to, um. I mean, now and again he'll do things for me but he's always, oh [exhales] you know, and a moan and a groan and, you know.

While Liz is prepared to 'shove' Adam, ensuring he fulfils obligations and takes up opportunities, she is anxious that this approach encourages his laziness. By taking an indirect responsibility for her son's life decisions, she is worried that he is not developing the independence and self-sufficiency he will need to carry him through his adult life. Nevertheless, Liz is clear that laziness is considerably preferable to the risks associated with her reduced input. Liz's account of parenting reveals the amount of effort and commitment she feels mothering requires. Yet the emotional labour she undertakes is largely invisible and directed towards aims that are less likely to be understood or shared by the middle classes. Her deep sense of personal responsibility for the actions, choices and decisions made by her children is primarily orientated towards protecting them from the pitfalls and uncertainties of a dangerous world. With middle-class children considerably more insulated from these risks, their parents can afford to centre their emotional investments on conserving and consolidating their advantages. Middle-class perspectives are often unable to recognise the particular strengths and benefits of working-class parenting practices, and are liable to misinterpret this emotional investment in terms of low aspiration and lack of concern.

Gender, commitment and mothering

> Being a good mum comes from being a good person, and you've got to be a good person to be a good mum.
>
> (Sam – white, working-class mother)

As I have argued, the notion that working-class mothers are uncaring or indifferent to their children's needs pervades our culture. Such mothers are often set against 'ideal' models depicting 'sensitive' attunement to children's developmental needs. Nevertheless, the working-class mothers discussed in this book are heavily invested in traditional gendered constructions of motherhood in terms of commitment, devotion and dedication. Other research also suggests that those publicly constructed as a threat to the stability of the family are the most likely to draw on traditional views about the role of women and set particularly high standards for themselves as mothers (Bullen *et al.* 2000). Being a 'good mother' is inextricably bound up with wider, moral evaluations of the self. Arguably, no other role or status of existence so comprehensively determines notions of social and personal worth for women. However, the powerful meaning and value attached to motherhood leave very little space to articulate personal hopes or desires.

As Steph Lawler (2000) has pointed out, 'good' mothers are presented as having no needs beyond those which are functional for the child, therefore children are portrayed as having 'needs' while mothers are seen only as experiencing 'wants'. The working-class women featured in this book all accepted primary responsibility for the care of their children, expressing appreciation where fathers were involved, or resigned disapproval where they were not. Very different standards were applied to describe motherhood as opposed to fatherhood, revealing the powerful moral codes constraining the women's actions and decisions. As the case study example of Sarah demonstrates, a perceived failure to live up to high standards of selfless engagement can provoke guilt-ridden confessions.

Sarah explained how she met Tony while she was still at school. A few years older than her, he was working at a local garage and mixing in a similar social circle. They went out for a number of years and decided to save to buy a house together. She described how they struggled for five years to get the deposit money together for a mortgage, scrimping and saving every last penny. Sarah worked in a shoe shop at the time, and was only paying a small amount of 'keep' to her mother and stepfather, but she found it difficult to meet the ambitious saving targets Tony had set. She described how this was the source of much argument between them and acknowledges that the deposit money primarily came from Tony's (significantly higher) wages. Eventually they moved into a small two-bedroom house, and struggled to pay the monthly mortgage in the face of rising interest rates. Sarah left her job at the shoe shop for better paid shift work on a production line and Tony took on regular overtime. After a couple of years they felt financially secure enough to try for a baby, and Sarah became pregnant straight away.

Sarah described Lisa as a 'good baby' for the first six weeks, until she started getting extended bouts of colic. Lisa stopped sleeping and began crying incessantly, placing a serious strain on Sarah and Tony. Although Sarah felt that Tony was initially supportive, he was working as a garage mechanic during the day and would sleep through Lisa's cries at night. Sarah described how she became depressed a few months after Lisa's birth, finding it difficult to adjust to the lack of sleep and the social isolation. She had previously worked in a factory making sweets and had desperately missed the regular company of the other women on her section. She also described her initial reluctance to take Lisa out when she was a baby in case her inexperience as a mother attracted disapproval or even suspicion from on-lookers. Sarah remembered how, at the time, other new mothers had seemed considerably more confident and competent. Although she eventually settled into motherhood, Sarah's relationship with Tony became increasingly fraught and volatile over the years. She described how they argued constantly, particularly over money. Tony kept tight control over their finances, providing Sarah with a limited allowance each month for shopping. Sarah described how she would walk miles with Lisa to find the cheapest super-market but would still run out of money by the end of the month. She often resorted to 'swiping' money and cigarettes out of Tony's pockets when he wasn't looking.

Sarah met Chris whilst visiting an old school friend in Greece, on a two-week break which had been arranged as a family holiday until Tony's boss became ill and needed him to take care of the business. Sarah and Lisa went without Tony, and met Chris, a close friend of the family they were staying with. Sarah began a passionate relationship with Chris, facilitated by her friend, who babysat Lisa. Sarah described how meeting Chris changed her life, making her determined to leave Tony and 'start a new life'. She spent an unhappy few months after coming home, and eventually decided to tell Tony about Chris, and return to Greece. She left Lisa with Tony for five weeks, arranging for Lisa to join her for the last two weeks of her stay. Meanwhile Chris decided to apply for a work visa and move to the UK.

Sarah returned from Greece with £100 provided by Chris, and with the intention of finding somewhere for herself and Lisa to live. Having managed to get hold of another hundred pounds ('swiped' from Tony's pocket), she moved into a room, a few streets away from Tony, rented from a friend of her mother's, and claimed housing benefit. Tony, however, refused to let Lisa move in with Sarah, claiming the room was too small and dirty for a child to live in. While she was angry and frustrated, Sarah could see his point. Sarah describes this as particularly bleak period of her life, lightened only by time spent with Lisa and occasional visits from Chris. She explained how she became quite ill psychologically and began taking anti-depressants.

During this time Tony was also finding it difficult caring for Lisa while also holding down a full-time job as a mechanic. He relied heavily on Sarah and her mother for practical support, but found basic chores like cooking and cleaning a huge strain. Sarah knew Tony wanted her back, but she felt angry and determined. She moved in with her mother and insisted that as part-owner of the house she was due some money from Tony. She explained to him that she would use it to rent a flat for herself and Lisa close by, and he reluctantly agreed to give her £1,000. Sarah found a one-bedroom flat a few streets away from Tony, and it was agreed that Lisa would spend the weekdays with her mother and the weekends with her father. Sarah had been dismayed by the shortfall between the weekly rent and the maximum housing benefit she was entitled to, but Tony had agreed to pay the difference, for the time being. From Sarah's point of view, moving into the flat provided her with an opportunity to start again and build a new, more stable home life for Lisa.

Sarah gave a highly confessional account of these events, with actions and events described in terms of their negative impact on Lisa. Although Sarah remained intimately involved with her daughter's day-to-day life, she contravened her personal understandings of good motherhood by leaving in the first place. Although she sought to explain and justify her actions, her account was dominated by expressions of concern and regret that Lisa had suffered as a result:

> I decided that I was going to split up with her dad. And I went away on holiday and left her here. I think that affected her as well. Um, even though she had a lot of support from my mother, um, I think that really sort . . . 'Cos I went away for seven weeks and then she came, she came. I went abroad, I went to Greece and, um, she came out for the last two weeks of my stay, and it was quite difficult 'cos of the language barrier, even though I'd learnt a bit of language. I think she found it quite difficult, but I mean, then when we came back after Christmas. Of course I wasn't around Christmas as well, so that probably affected her, it was probably the first time she'd never spent Christmas with Mum. Because Tony wanted her to be there for Christmas, which is understandable I suppose.

Sarah became emotionally distressed when she described being apart from Lisa at Christmas. She felt the symbolism of leaving her daughter at this time was too painful to discuss and clearly felt considerable guilt about having made the decision to go. Sarah's guilt was compounded by her sense that she had failed to live up to her own standards from the start. She explained how giving birth to Lisa had been a traumatic experience. She had felt out of control, overwhelmed by pain and fear and bullied by unsympathetic nurses. Her description of this was predominantly conveyed through humour, with an emphasis placed on the unreasonable abuse she heaped on Tony for getting her pregnant in the first place. But her story of Lisa's birth was also underpinned by anger, indignation and guilt. She explained how the nurse in charge had been rough and domineering, and had seemed unmoved by her real distress. Sarah explained how, in her exhausted despair after the birth, she told the nurses she no longer wanted the baby, shocking them, Tony and herself. While Sarah laughed as she described the farcical nature of this incident, she was clearly still disturbed by her initial rejection of her daughter. She emphasised how deeply mortified she felt afterwards, and explained how, during rows, Tony often maliciously reminded her that she'd asked the nurses to take Lisa away straight after she'd been born.

Sarah was particularly regretful about her perceived inability to provide Lisa with what she termed a 'proper childhood', and she drew on a very traditional model of family to highlight her daughter's loss:

> What would you say is a proper childhood?
>
> Tracy, my friend Tracy, she's what you call a proper mum.

So what's that then?

Someone who's, you know, always there in the kitchen. [He] works normal hours. The dad's got a good job. She, she, and I would say Tina as well, Tina's, you know, having a nice home. It's having a mum and a dad. But then I suppose with Tina and her husband, he's a fireman and he's hardly ever there. Um, but with, it just seems to be that is more, would probably be, is more stable. You know, is more roots there than having one big upheaval and arguments and rows and, and moving house and home.

The link Sarah makes between having a 'proper childhood' and having a 'proper mum' undermines her own status as a mother. A 'proper mum' provides a 'proper childhood' by being 'always there in the kitchen', a role Sarah has been unable and unwilling to sustain. From Sarah's perspective, authentic motherhood also appears to require a father with a good job to ensure material security and a 'nice home', resources she relinquished when she left Tony. However, despite this ideal construction of 'proper' mother-hood, Sarah is mindful of the impossible standards it appears to demand. She reflected that the negative impact on Lisa began long before she left, and highlighted the gap between representations of happy families and reality as it is lived:

Arguments, she'd seen me get upset. Um, I'd been crying. And then we got a dog and that was horrible, wrecked the joint. Basically she just saw that, that I was unhappy all the time and her father was unhappy all the time, and I don't think she really knew what totally was going on . . . I think when two people can't get on, and when two people find that things have gone out of control and then you go a bit peculiar in the head, it's a bit hard to be normal and behave and act like the way these books say you should behave. You just really do your best.

Did you read books, then?

No [laughs]. But I know that, say, what is it, um, the reason, well actually I did actually, umm, before Lisa was born, and when she was

> born I think I read loads of books. It looks very, it all looks good down on paper but behaviour, you'd have to be a robot, to be honest. Not a computer but a robot to be able to. Because people are human and they're not. It's not all this rose cottage covered house and lovely back garden and swing and slide and dog and cat and [puts on an affected voice] 'Hello daring, had a lovely day at work? [laughs]. Oh and how was your day, and oh dinner smells nice', and you know, all that crap.

Sarah clearly feels she has let her daughter down, but she is also angry at having invested in an unrealistic and ultimately unobtainable ideal. Some of the other mothers in the sample expressed a similar bitterness, but preserved their moral status by retaining full-time care of their children. For Sarah, leaving her daughter with her father (albeit for a short period) represents an inexcusable breech of motherhood, symbolising her previous standing as a 'bad mother'. This reveals the extent to which lives are constrained historically and culturally, specific orthodoxies delimiting and regulating the experience of being a mother.

The women in this study had consciously sought to become mothers and live up to the ideals of commitment associated with this social role, but this inevitably entailed a relinquishment of self-interest for a focus on the 'needs' of their children. While many gained a powerful sense of satisfaction and self-worth from being a 'good mother', this positive identity could not be enjoyed without considerable sacrifice and struggle. Investment in the discourse of motherhood left little opportunity to articulate personal desires, and any actions which could be interpreted as compromising a child's best interest were warranted within a framework prioritising children's needs, or were painfully regretted. As Steph Lawler (2000) notes of children's needs:

> These discourses are fundamentally depoliticizing in their simultaneous inclusion of, and denial of, class, gender and 'race'. In theory, they propose, anyone can meet children's needs; it is 'parenting skills', rather than social (dis)advantage which counts. In practice, only certain, socially advantaged, families are understood as adequately meeting their children's needs.
>
> (Lawler 2000: 139)

The example of Sarah highlights in particular the profoundly gendered nature of parenthood. While the mothers in this study negotiate boundaries between their personal subjectivity and motherhood differently, all are positioned and contained by gendered assumptions and the lack power associated with them. Had Sarah been a man she would have an accepted claim to the status of 'good father' on the grounds of enduring concern and contact. As many have noted, fathers regard themselves, and can be regarded as 'good fathers' while remaining relatively distant from the physical practice of childrearing (Gillies 2006c; Phoenix and Woollett 1991). Being a mother, on the other hand, is constructed in terms of commitment, devotion and dedication, and is closely associated with moral worth. It is also associated with a financial vulnerability which severely restricts life choices, as Sarah's case illustrates. Lack of money and cramped, temporary housing conditions severely constrained Sarah's role as a mother, preventing her from caring for Lisa in a full-time capacity, as she had planned to do:

> And that was, so she wasn't living with me, she was living with Tony, and I, which was very upsetting because I didn't, I only had her at weekends and that was, that was a strain because I was living with someone and I had all these suitcases and one little room on me own and, ohhhh it was horrible. And then things got really bad and me mum said I could move in with her, so that made things a bit easier. Just a bit more stable. 'Cos where I was living, Lisa couldn't stay there if she wanted to because I didn't think it would have been . . . 'cos the woman was unstable herself.

Sarah's guilt-ridden account conveys her perceived sense of failure, but it also reveals her strength, determination and sense of responsibility as a mother. Lisa was carefully planned in the context of a financially stable partnership, and Sarah's experience of isolation and financial dependence is attributed to Tony's unreasonable behaviour rather than an inevitable consequence of motherhood. While Sarah left to visit Chris in Greece, she had no intention of relinquishing custody of her daughter. This commitment shaped and constrained her decisions leading her to return to the UK and seek a home for herself and Lisa. The financial difficulties she encountered sabotaged this effort and resulted in her losing full-time care of her daughter. Although not living under the same roof, Sarah spent considerable time with her daughter during this period, and with the help of her mother made sure she was properly fed and had clean clothes for school.

Sarah's struggle to gain economic independence highlights the bleak prospects facing women attempting to escape abusive relationships. While Sarah was eventually able to negotiate a financial contribution from Tony that allowed her to mother Lisa full time, women in more dangerous situations are often forced to rely on the limited help provided by refuges. Sarah's account also illustrates the enormous significance of home. Without a home, Sarah felt unable to mother. Securing a flat of her own allowed her to look positively to the future and focus on repairing some of the damage she feels was inflicted on Lisa. A defining feature of Sarah's story is her relief and satisfaction in now being able to live up to her own standards of good motherhood.

Conclusion: valuing working-class mothering

The chapter has explored the rich cultural and emotional resources provided by working-class mothers. The women in this study attached a powerful significance to motherhood and cared deeply about their children. Their commitment and sense of responsibility was often characterised by personal sacrifice and struggle, yet also generated great pleasure and satisfaction. This was demonstrated by Sam's account of lone motherhood, and also the case study example of Kelly, who remained dedicated to her children through violence, vulnerability and extreme poverty, and continued to cope with serious and stressful after-effects on her son. Kelly's strength and competence is unrecognised in her interactions with professionals, while her family's more pressing needs for practical support go unmet. The abject status of working-class mothers ensures the crucial resources they provide are at best overlooked and at worst pathologised. Recognition of this labour would demand an appreciation of the varied and situated roles that parents play in caring for their children. I have suggested that the concept of 'emotional capital' can help to illuminate the classed nature of parenting practices, revealing a contrast between middle-class preoccupations with academic performance and working-class concerns to keep children safe, soothe feelings of failure and low self-worth, and challenge injustice. In the context of poverty, vulnerability and failure, working-class children may have precious few resources to draw on other than the emotional capital they access from their mothers.

Stereotypes of indifferent, uncaring parents are highly gendered as well as classed, and this is illustrated by the case study example of Sarah. Relinquishing custody of her child, albeit unintentionally and for a short period, is perceived by Sarah to be unforgivable, and she is determined to build a new safe, secure home from which to repair any damage suffered by her daughter. Sarah's experiences reveal the way motherhood is inextricably linked to self-worth for women, inspiring guilt and anxiety alongside pleasure and fulfilment. The determination and resilience evident in Sarah's account is common to all the mothers in this study. Caring for children was prioritised and highly valued in the context of hardship, struggle and disrespect. Few perceived themselves to be particularly oppressed or dwelt on their difficulties or deprivations. As Beverley Skeggs notes, working-class women are more likely to refuse victimhood, cover up injury, and endure to display that they can cope (2005: 971). Nevertheless, as I argue in the final chapter, these women and their children deserve far more than they get in terms of respect and resources.

Chapter 7

Situating understandings of mothering

Issues and implications

> Perhaps there is little understanding of the ways in which the middle-class approach to child rearing intertwines with the dominant ideology of our society, making the idea that a middle-class childhood might not be the optimal approach literally unthinkable.
>
> (Lareau 2003: 65)

This book has explored the lives and experiences of working-class mothers. More specifically it has sought to demonstrate how decisions and practices which make less sense from a middle-class vantage point shift their meaning when viewed from a specific, situated working-class perspective. The day-to-day challenges facing these mothers have been described in terms of their ongoing struggles to cope with financial constraint, vulnerability, insecurity, limited power and disrespect. The extent to which this material and social reality generates values and practices that are distinct from normative middle-class expectations has also been discussed. For the mothers featured in this book, individualistic principles taken for granted by the by the middle classes were more likely to be experienced in terms of isolation, marginalisation and pathologisation. Most had little to gain and much more to lose from emphasising their own or their children's exceptionality as more privileged middle-class parents do. Instead they tended to display a greater relational sense of self, de-centring personal interest and stressing the inter-dependency of a family that often included friends.

The mothers also drew protective boundaries between home and school, constructing family life as a crucial refuge from the dangers and stresses of the outside world. Education was viewed as an external activity entrusted to teachers, while the mothers focus on loving, protecting and caring for their children. In maintaining these home–school boundaries, the mothers were able to create a nurturing space in which to soothe the injuries and injustices of class. They generated valuable emotional capital, enabling their children to survive the 'symbolic violence' (Bourdieu and Passeron 1977) perpetrated by the education system. At times the mothers found themselves in direct confrontation with middle-class professionals, fighting hard for their children's rights. Lack of power and influence could provoke extreme reactions from the mothers, but a forceful or aggressive response often produced more satisfaction, both emotionally and practically, than composed attempts to negotiate on middle-class terms.

But perhaps the most significant point illuminated by this book is the extent to which these working-class mothers value, and are committed to, child-rearing. While most endured great personal sacrifice to parent, it was rarely perceived in these terms. Emphasis was placed on pleasure, satisfaction and achievement, with little time spent dwelling on deprivations or unfulfilled desires. In this last chapter, I place this portrait of working-class mothers' lives in a broader context to consider issues of morality and social justice. I begin with a discussion of the ways in which dominant middle-class discourses might construct the mothers featured in this book as lacking, unskilled and irresponsible. I draw out the inherent contradictions running through sanctioned parenting models and show how alternative working-class approaches carry an equally persuasive moral logic. I will then turn to the policy implications that stem from this research. I call for a new approach that recognises the validity and strengths of working-class mothering, while also addressing the ingrained inequity that frames their experiences and practices. In short, I make the case for replacing coercive 'skills' training and other forms of regulation with real financial, practical and material support.

Working-class parenting through a middle-class lens

As I have argued, constructions childhood and children's needs are presented and imposed as if they were natural and universal, placing pressure on all mothers to justify their actions within a sanctioned model of child development. Yet normative expectations around childrearing are for the most part grounded in middle-class privilege, with this crucial social and material context obscured by a focus on development and parenting practices. Interpretations of what children are and need patently reflect a white, middle-class cultural hegemony. Parenting practice has always varied across cultures. For example, the Western convention of mother as primary care taker and father as breadwinner does not extend to other societies in which children are cared for by a number of different adults in the community (Seymour 1999; Hill Collins 1990).

Furthermore, dominant constructions of childhood as fragile, passive, dependent, and in need of continuity and protection within 'stable' two-parent families can be contrasted with other cultures in which childhood is very differently defined. In many developing countries children are required through necessity to work from an early age, and as a consequence Western understandings of childhood as special and distinct from adulthood simply cannot be afforded. While there is often talk of securing 'children's rights' in developing countries, concern is more predominantly focused on upholding a particular notion of childhood rather than challenging the economic conditions that generate oppressive, exploitative labour conditions for children and adults (Boyden 1990). Similarly, in the UK efforts to support children's development more commonly involve attempts to promote middle-class parenting without providing the access to resources that underpin such approaches.

It is often taken for granted that children need security, stability and safety in order to thrive, and assumed that parents have a responsibility to provide this. Yet as I have shown, parenting cannot transcend socio-economic reality. The mothers featured in this book struggled with hardship and uncertainty, while actively fighting to make their own and their children's lives better. All conveyed a strong sense of vulnerability, investing a great deal of energy in consolidating their gains by putting a 'floor' on their circumstances (Skeggs 1997). Considerable mental and physical effort was put in into retaining basic resources and preventing backward slippage, but these mothers were simply unable to ensure that their children grew up without experiencing and understanding deprivation. As Jane Ribbens (1994) notes, mothers are expected to walk a tightrope, upholding the purity and innocence of childhood, while also ensuring their children develop towards efficacy and self-sufficiency of adulthood (Ribbens 1994). This task is particularly tricky for working-class mothers who might feel torn between protecting children from everyday worries and threats and making sure they are streetwise and resilient.

Such parenting decisions, practices and aspirations can only be understood in their situated context. For working-class children instability, struggle and unfulfilled desire are unavoidable facets of life. Coming to terms with disappointment, frustration and vulnerability represents a vital feature of growing up, and is therefore a key responsibility of working-class parenting. In contrast, the continuity and security that is likely to characterise a middle-class childhood will in all probability continue into adult life. In this sense parents from different social classes are oriented towards very different projects in raising their children. While working-class mothers aim to pass on resilience and coping skills, middle-class mothers are seeking to pass on privilege and sense of entitlement. A common lack of understanding of these different challenges and orientations ensure that value-laden interpretations of working-class parenting practices dominate. Working-class mothers may be portrayed as harsh, lacking in warmth and authoritarian if they fail to inculcate values which they might perceive as actively undermining their family life. As I have demonstrated, middle-class practices which foreground democracy and negotiation are risky in a context where choice and power are limited, hazards are many and consequences severe.

Dominant child-centred discourses depend on a view of children as developing individuals and parents as facilitators. This particular construction of 'child' is universalised and essentialised as a prior category against which normative evaluations of mothering rest (Lawler 1999). Chris Jenks (1996) has analysed the multiple and often contradictory meanings associated with childhood over the centuries. He identifies two distinct conceptualisations that have characterised representations of children and childcare across history. The first is what Jenks terms the 'Dionysian image'. From this viewpoint children are regarded as a wilful, hedonistic force, mischievous and bent on seeking pleasure. The second is the 'Apollonian image', which views the child as angelic, pure and innocent, possessing an innate potential and capacity for goodness. Jenks demonstrates how these representations highlight the 'shifting strategies that Western society has exercised in its increasing need to control, socialise and constrain people in the transition towards modernity' (1996: 74). While strands of both images may be identified at different times and in different contexts, they reveal a particular understanding of social organisation. The Dionysian child reflects a rule-based, external view of society in which subjects must be disciplined into consensual conformity, while the Apollonian child represents a more individualised internalisation of surveillance through an ideology of personal development.

Contemporary policy discourse spans both of these constructions of children, in what amounts to class-specific interpretations. Child-centred 'Apollonian' perspectives, stressing the need for sensitive attention to the developing child's needs, is reflected in institutionalised middle-class standards by which working-class mothers are judged as wanting. Working-class children, however, are more likely to be described in 'Dionysian' terms as wild, hedonistic and in need of civilising. While a normal (middle-class) child requires stimulation and encouragement to learn, problem (working-class) children need to be watched, disciplined and controlled. Policy initiatives straddle both approaches, holding up the 'Apollonian' child as the model promoted by parenting classes and the 'Dionysian' child as evidence of a failure which may necessitate criminal justice procedure.

Consequently, while parenting classes are being rolled out across the country, anti-social behaviour orders (ASBOs) are simultaneously being issued, at an alarming rate. ASBOs were introduced as part of the Crime and Disorder Act (1988) and ban individuals from undertaking certain activities or entering particular geographical areas. Designed as part of the UK government's agenda to promote respect, half of all ASBOs have been issued to children (Rowlands 2005). In specific cases they have been used to criminalise ball games, certain terms of abuse, socialising and wearing particular items of clothes, as well as other non-criminal activities. Statistics from the Youth Justice Board show that nearly 50 young people were taken into custody for breaching an ASBO in any month in 2004 (see www.asbocon cern.org.uk). This policy direction reveals the thin line dividing government efforts to 'support' and enable, from a more authoritarian instinct towards coercion and regulation. It also highlights major tensions characterising state-sanctioned childrearing models.

Contradictions of individualism

Underpinning contemporary value-laden middle-class interpretations of parenting practices is an attachment to liberal individualism as an undisputed given. But as Billig and colleagues (1988) note, individualism represents an inherently contradictory ideology, encompassing contrasting themes of individual freedom and personal responsibility. This tension is clearly visible in the UK New Labour government's so called 'third way' approach, which seeks a communitarian influenced solution to perceived deficit parenting and its threat to social cohesion. Appeals to the common social good are made through the morally charged language of individualism which emphasises parental obligation to raise appropriate subjects. The more relational experience of self described by the mothers in this book is not recognised or valued. Instead, working-class parents are represented as both too selfish and not individualised enough to ensure the normal development of their children.

This focus on 'normal' development highlights a further contradiction. Dominant models of childrearing promote a 'concerted cultivation' approach, requiring sustained and substantial input from parents (Lareau 2003). Natural growth is not enough. Emerging individuality must be tamed, shaped and fashioned to ensure that children become the right kind of selves. They can be facilitated to fulfil their personal potential only through particular interventions and within certain parameters. In this sense, measures of normal development represent not what children generally are, but instead what their parents should aim for them to become. From this perspective, working-class mothers who value their children as individuals regardless of their achievements are condemned for lacking aspiration and commitment. Meanwhile, the academic development of middle-class children is prioritised and justified through claims of exceptionality, natural ability and deservingness.

Furthermore, as Steph Lawler (2000) argues, the normative categorisation of children as both the same and yet different has profound consequences for those positioned as 'other'. As she explains:

> Euroamerican understandings of children are dominated by a fundamental contradiction: all children are the same – they pass through the same developmental 'milestones', they exhibit the same fundamental characteristics, they have the same 'needs'. At the same time, all children are held to be unique. The 'uniqueness' of children is a manifestation of the uniqueness and individuality which Western selves are supposed

to inhabit . . . but what must be noted is that this forced commonality
rests upon a violence – the exclusion of those who stand outside of its
charmed circle.

(Lawler 2000: 40)

This contradictory discourse of individualism originates from and benefits
the middle classes (Skeggs 1997). For the working-class mothers in this book,
any exceptionality of their children was more likely to be experienced in
terms of exclusion. The mothers feared the consequences of their children
standing out as the 'wrong' sort of individual and were concerned to ensure
that they blended in with others. Again, this desire for their children to avoid
being singled out as 'special' is commonly misinterpreted as indicating
low aspiration and lack of interest. There is little recognition of the way in
which the status of legitimate individual is restricted to those with access to
the right sort of cultural capital. Middle-class children are viewed as entitled
individuals, whereas when working-class children are individualised they are
invariably marked out as a problem.

Yet in terms of inequality and disadvantage, individualism is commonly
portrayed as both the problem and solution. There is no conception that
people might experience themselves as anything other than self-interested
individuals. The cultural hegemony of individualism is manifest in the angst-
ridden nature of contemporary social commentary. The individualisation
associated with late capitalism is viewed by many as having pervaded the
domestic sphere and corrupted the way in which intimate social relations
are experienced (Fevre 2000; Lasch 1977; Sennett 1998). Such concerns are
articulated by politicians through a focus on the individual morals and
behaviour of the working class, who are seen as unable to meet the challenges
of individualisation. Despite strong evidence to the contrary, poverty and
disadvantage is regularly explained in terms of isolation from traditional
support structures in an increasingly atomised society (Everingham 2003).

From the perspective of policy-makers, middle-class parents are seen as
competent in cultivating social networks that they can draw on to the advantage of themselves and their children. Conversely, a deficit of links to the
local community is viewed as a problem of disadvantaged areas where
there is a high dependency on the welfare state and a perceived lack of self-
sufficiency. Over the past few years, UK policy initiatives have focused on
building 'social capital' in an attempt re-socialise the poor (Gewirtz 2001;
Gillies 2005a). Broadly defined as values that people hold and the resources
that they can access through collective social relationships, social capital is
viewed in terms of networks characterised by shared values and social bonds
that benefit individuals and society (Edwards *et al.* 2003). This approach to
social capital differs significantly from Bourdieu's interpretation of it as
inextricably linked to economic, cultural and symbolic capital, and playing
a key role in the class-specific perpetuation of inequality.

As Christine Everingham (2003) suggests, mainstream policy interpretations of social capital often rely on a circular argument in which poverty derives from lack of social capital and lack of social capital derives from poverty. This circular logic has spawned a myriad of policy remedies focused on helping the poor generate social relations that will benefit themselves and their families. Such an instrumental approach to social relations requires a highly individualistic ethos at odds with the emotionally intense bonds created by working-class mothers. As I discussed in Chapter 4, mothers with few needs or obligations tend to be attached to the kinds of networks envisaged by policy-makers. Less privileged mothers form inter-dependent relationships that stand in contrast to individualistic middle-class values. There is little recognition that these crucial reciprocal social networks may be sustained precisely because of a lack of self-interest and instrumentalism. Individualism is a risky value system for working-class families. Not only does it expose and exclude those unable to construct themselves as legitimate selves, it also threatens relational ties and support systems (Gillies and Edwards 2006).

Challenging orthodoxies

In spite of the situated and class-specific nature of parenting, the current UK government seems increasingly determined to valorise and enforce particular childrearing strategies and values. They have displayed an almost evangelical faith in the power of parenting to compensate for social disadvantage. This is reflected in the strident tones of Margaret Hodge, the Minister for Children who, in response to concerns about the government overstepping its bounds and interfering, stated: 'For me it's not a question of whether we should intrude in family life, but how and when' (speech to the IPPR, 26 November 2004).

Discussions have been conducted over the last few years about the introduction of a 'Parents' Code', in which the rights and responsibilities of parents would be clearly defined, detailing the practices and values that parents are expected to adhere to and informing 'a national consciousness of what it is to be a parent' (Henricson 2003: 94). As Madeleine Bunting (2004) argues, this preoccupation with parenting has brought a whole new meaning to the phrase 'the personal is political':

> What the [political] right always does is to make the structural effects of disadvantage, deprivation and alienation the personal responsibility of poor parents. If there is crime or low educational achievement, it's the fault of inadequate parenting rather than the result of political and economic failure. New Labour wouldn't make that mistake. But, crucially, it follows a similar logic of putting the responsibility on to

parents to break cycles of deprivation through the sheer force of their parenting skills. It won't raise benefit levels to ensure parents and their children are not living in poverty, it won't intervene in the economy to ensure jobs, but it will offer courses on how to play with your child.

More significantly, 'good parenting' is discussed by the government as if it were objectively definable rather than value driven. This conceals the contested nature of the principles and objectives that underpin sanctioned models of childrearing, particularly in terms of definitions of success and failure. The philosophy of 'concerted cultivation' (Lareau 2003) structuring institutionally approved methods of parenting prioritises achievement, competitiveness, self-conviction and instrumentalism. While these ideals may be advantageous to a capitalist society, they are stressed at the expense of alternative values such as self-acceptance, interdependence, kindness and humility. When stripped back to this level, pronouncements on parenting are revealed as highly contentious. Far from the mainstream consensus implied by the government, debates continue to rage over the values that should inform childrearing.

For example, concern is often expressed about middle-class children who are under constant pressure from their parents and teachers to perform. In their longitudinal study of young women born in the 1970s, Valerie Walkerdine and colleagues (2001) highlight the way fear of failure in middle-class families provokes feelings of inadequacy, insecurity and guilt among middle-class girls. Similarly, Helen Lucey and Diane Reay's (2002) focus on secondary school transfer examines the emotional consequences of a sustained stress on progression and success:

> For the middle-class children, failure is simply not an available option and they are under intense pressure to succeed educationally. It is also becoming increasingly clear that only very high levels of attainment are good enough. The government definition of 'exam success' at GCSE (5 GCSEs at grades A–C) would be considered by most professional middle-class families as not just mediocre, but a failure (Walkerdine *et al.* 2001). This level of attainment is certainly not good enough to ensure a place at a 'good' university. For girls in particular, their high performance produced and was produced *within* an emotional dilemma in which they struggled with feelings of not being good enough, alongside equally powerful feelings of not being allowed to fail.
>
> (Lucey and Reay 2002: 10)

These experiences are produced within the framework of the ongoing assessment regime that school pupils in the UK are subject to. Children currently sit Standard Assessment Tests (SATs) at ages 7, 11 and 14, and before their General Certificate of Secondary Education (GCSE) examinations at 16. While the government emphasises the importance of setting targets and maintaining educational standards, research points to the serious impact this can have on pupils' psychological wellbeing. In a survey of parents conducted for the *Times Education Supplement*, it was found that one in ten 7-year-old children had been reduced to tears and lost sleep due to anxiety over SATs. In addition, 34 per cent of 11-year-olds were said to be suffering from general stress, a quarter were reported as having lost their confidence, while one-fifth were said to regularly prioritise revising over playing with friends (*EducationGuardian* 2003). These findings are further contextualised by an apparent sharp rise in emotional and behavioural problems among children over the last 25 years (Collishaw *et al.* 2004). While there may be much disagreement about the causes of this alleged rise, uncritical adoption by the state of concerted cultivation as the gold standard of childrearing is at the very least open to question.

Furthermore, in her ethnography of family life in the US, Annette Lareau (2003) identifies a number of distinct disadvantages associated with the concerted cultivation approach taken by many middle-class parents. She reports that the lives of middle-class children she studied were often characterised by a hectic pace, dictated by tightly scheduled educational and leisure activities. They had little time to relax or engage in unstructured play and often complained of being tired. She also observed that they appeared to lack the enthusiasm and excitement displayed by their working-class counterparts. Larueu notes that middle-class children often complained of boredom and seemed underwhelmed by the opportunities and resources they were provided with. In contrast, working-class children appeared to derive much pleasure from their leisure activities of socialising and playing. They also eagerly looked forward to simple treats such as attending a family party or having pizza for dinner.

Nevertheless, Annette Lareau acknowledges the very real, material advantages that concerted cultivation as a childrearing strategy confers upon middle-class children. The synchronicity of this approach with institutional values reaps considerable benefits in terms of academic attainment, while also fostering instrumentalism and a sense of entitlement. However, as I have sought to demonstrate in this book, working-class children and their parents may have more to lose than gain from adhering to a philosophy of concerted cultivation. Aside from the obvious fact that disadvantaged mothers are unable to access the economic, social and cultural resources to shape their children as middle-class selves, inculcating the necessary values may be a difficult and risky enterprise for such parents. While for middle-class children there may be many cultural similarities between school, home and leisure activities, working-class children require wide-ranging skills to safely span institutional and personal worlds. Individualistic middle-class values around achievement, competition, entitlement and instrumentalism might be read by peers as evidence of self-centeredness, conceit, disloyalty or personal exploitation. Vulnerable working-class families cannot afford to risk the social alienation this might provoke. Perhaps more importantly, many working-class mothers are appalled by these values themselves.

Alternative moral logics

The practices of the working-class mothers discussed in this book were guided by an alternative moral framework grounded in personal and social experience. Yet the institutional dominance of the concerted cultivation approach, combined with a policy emphasis on rationality and responsibility, ensures there is little space for the recognition of contrasting values. Instead, the ethical world views of these mothers are de-legitimised and ignored in a rush to construct a moral vacuum at the heart of their parenting practices. As Andrew Sayer (2005) suggests, there is a tendency for such formal accounts of human behaviour to describe and explain without considering the significance of emotional meaning. As he states:

> In order to understand our normative orientation to the world we therefore need to avoid treating fact and value, reason and emotion, as opposed, and acknowledge that while emotions and values are fallible they are not irrational or 'merely subjective', but are often perceptive and reasonable judgements about situations and processes.
>
> (Sayer 2005: 951)

The normative orientation of the working-class mothers in this book diverged from middle-class childrearing expectations on a number of issues. But these alternative views are rarely even heard, let alone understood. The marginalised and largely invisible nature of these working-class perspectives attract accusations of ignorance and amorality, which disintegrate under sustained examination. For example, the mothers were deeply concerned about issues of petty crime and 'anti-social behaviour', not least because they and their family had often fallen victim to it. Even those mothers with children in trouble with the police or teachers assumed a moral position condemning the bad behaviour in question, while sometimes also refuting allegations or emphasising mitigating circumstances. The caricature of the lazy, indifferent 'pramface' impassively letting her children run wild could not be further from the truth. Discipline and good behaviour were highly valued traits, and the mothers were acutely aware of the dangers, bad influences and temptations surrounding their children. In this fraught context, middle-class values around negotiation and democracy could actively undermine efforts to enforce and maintain parental control. Annette Lareau's (2003) and Walkerdine et al.'s (2001) observation that middle-class children who are encouraged to reason and negotiate can become defiant and rude, highlights the dangers of this approach for working-class parents. Yet by ignoring the orthodoxy of sensitive parenting, working-class mothers are vulnerable to accusations that they are authoritarian and lacking in warmth.

The very different values that working-class mothers hold in relation to their children's development also need to be recognised in terms of a distinct moral logic guiding parenting practice. The mothers took enormous pride and pleasure in watching their children grow up and attached worth to a wide range of traits, characteristics and achievements. They were not fixated on increasing their children's intellectual capacity and were not engaged with measurement and assessment to insure developmental progress. On the contrary, the mothers emphasised the importance of non-academic qualities, thereby helping their children to cope with the emotional demands of school failure (Gillies 2006a). This is often read as a lack of parental support for children's education, leaving them with low aspirations and poor self-esteem. Yet, given that the odds are so firmly stacked against working-class children's academic success, placing strong value on educational achievement is likely to devastate the self-worth of the less successful majority. For many of the mothers themselves, the emotionally painful experience of failing at school was still fresh, and while they were keen to stress the benefits of education, they played down the personal significance low achievement.

As I have stated, the mothers viewed their role in terms of caring, protecting and loving their children rather than teaching or cultivating them. This stance is further contextualised by the power dynamics which characterise their experience of home–school relationships. By enforcing a 'cultural arbitrary' (Bourdieu and Passeron 1977), teachers were often viewed by the mothers as threatening the wellbeing of their children. The mothers described incidents where they felt their children had been sidelined or ignored, excluded or singled out as a problem, and/or put down and undermined. In these situations mothers acted out of concern and anger and were sometimes driven to extreme measures. They recognised and tolerated the higher value that teachers attached to 'bright' middle-class children and their parents, but they were determined to secure basic rights for their own children.

The conflict that often ensues between working-class parents and teachers is most commonly represented from a middle-class professional's point of view. Scare stories frequently appear in the media of unreasonable, aggressive parents intimidating and sometimes attacking teachers*. This stereotype of thuggish working-class parents was encapsulated in a speech given by

* See, for example, BBC News online 'Head teachers complain of abuse', Friday, 29 April, 2005 http://news.bbc.co.uk/1/hi/education/4493881.stm and 'Heads want power to expel children of violent parents' by Laura Clark, Daily Mail, 6 July 2005 http://www.daily-mail.co.uk/pages/live/articles/news/news.html?in_article_id=354792&in_page_id=1770

the former UK education minister Estelle Morris when she stressed the need to break the 'cycle of disrespect':

> There are too many instances of parents challenging a teacher's right to discipline their children according to the rules of the school. A message that has gone to that child is that teachers should not be respected and adults should not be respected, and that's not good enough.
>
> (Morris 2002)

The message here is clear: while middle-class parents can work in partnership with the school; working-class parents must know their place and respect the superiority of teachers. The lack of respect so often shown towards working-class parents and their children is rarely acknowledged. Instead, the anger and frustration displayed by parents is de-contextualised and treated as irrational, ignorant and delinquent. In their study of girls born in the 1970s, Valerie Walkerdine and colleagues (2001) provide an alternative perspective on the often poor relationship between working-class parents and teachers:

> For many of the working-class parents, their requests for help were forcefully blocked by the school, and we suggest that this could have had a powerful negative effect on their daughters in a number of ways. Firstly, of course, the special needs of the daughters were denied . . . Secondly, and perhaps more importantly in the longer term, the schools dismissal of the parents, and indeed of the parent's knowledge of the child, connected with the schools dismissal of the girls own abilities and knowledge. By dismissing the parent the teacher also dismissed the child.
>
> (Walkerdine *et al.* 2001: 130)

As this point demonstrates, simple narratives about working-class parents' unreasonable behaviour towards teachers may conceal a more complex and worrying situation. Yet for the most part interpretations of home–school relationships remain acutely insensitive to different experiences and ethical frameworks.

As I have shown, the mothers in this book demonstrated a clear moral logic guiding their interactions with teachers. While most were extremely tolerant and anxious to avoid trouble, they were also fiercely committed to protecting and preserving their children's wellbeing. The conflict they experienced with teachers and other middle-class professionals derived from a fundamental power imbalance which works to perpetuate the disadvantage experienced by working-class children. From this perspective, silence, withdrawal, anger, aggression and resistance are all justified and perfectly understandable reactions. As Simon Charlesworth argues, it is easy for those in a position of privilege to dismiss or overlook the injustice suffered by others.

> Complacency is part of the hidden benefits of privilege, and it is part of the mode of being-in-the-world that privilege fosters, and from this position the voices of those demanding redress always sound shrill, demanding, ugly.
>
> (Charlesworth 2000: 69)

Re-shaping policy debates

This book represents a clear challenge to the assumptions and objectives guiding contemporary family policy-making in the UK. First and foremost, it seriously undermines the notion that mothering skills are universal, easily abstracted and able to be neutrally conveyed in the form of parenting classes. It also strongly contests the claim that parenting practice is implicated in sustaining poverty. There is absolutely no evidence for this. Instead, by highlighting the resourceful and committed actions of marginalised mothers, I have shown how childrearing approaches inevitably reflect available family resources. Faith that further regulation of parenting will address issues of social exclusion and inequality appears to be based on little more than wishful thinking. This is underlined by the evaluation results of a number of major parenting programmes and initiatives such as Sure Start. These reveal that such interventions make little or no difference to disadvantage, and in some cases can even be harmful. Attempts to impose particular parenting practices and values ignore the grounded nature of childrearing, and thereby undermine the crucial situated strength and expertise of working-class mothers. Drawing on the work of Pierre Bourdieu (discussed in Chapter 2), it can be argued that the mothers' develop an embodied habitus that allows them to navigate the often gruelling demands and challenges that characterise their lives.

This book has also demonstrated how the ideal of parental involvement shaping contemporary education policy works to further compound inequality. The advantage middle-class parents pass on to their children depends on privileged access to money, high status social contacts, power and legitimated cultural knowledge (Gillies 2005b). Without acknowledgement of this uneven playing field, middle-class children's superior academic achievement is morally justified on the grounds of ability, hard work and appropriate parental nurturing. In contrast, working-class children are represented as being held back by unsupportive, insensitive and ignorant parents who don't deserve to see their children prosper.

Firmly grounded in a middle-class visibility and engagement with school structures, this model of parental involvement is unable to recognise the valuable contribution to children's education made by many working-class mothers. As I have shown, disadvantaged children require a different repertoire of skills, values and knowledge in comparison to their more privileged peers, and mothers play a crucial role in imparting these. Significantly, in their longitudinal, qualitative study, Valerie Walkerdine and colleagues (2001) found there to be no predictive power associated with the sanctioned 'sensitive mothering' approach. On the contrary, they found that some of the highest achieving girls had mothers that were, on these terms, defined as 'insensitive'.

Having critiqued existing policy aims and assumptions by stressing the situated and fundamentally classed nature of rationality and practice, I want to argue for an alternative approach that foregrounds issues of social justice for marginalised parents and their children. This would involve recognising and valuing working-class mothering while reasserting inequality as a moral issue. From this perspective, disadvantaged families of all kinds warrant respect for their ability to adapt to and cope with deprivation. More important, though, is recognising their deservingness of better financial, material and practical assistance to redress this fundamental injustice. This book has highlighted the serious gaps in state support and service provision encountered by working-class families. The mothers in this book were resourceful, creative and determined but were often denied basic requirements like a reasonable income, decent housing, safety and security and a fair education for their children.

In terms of income, the introduction of a tax credit system has undoubtedly raised living standards for many poor families. However, they also sustain insecure, low wage, 'flexible' working conditions requiring poor parents to undertake often menial and repetitive tasks for long hours for not a great deal more than they would receive in welfare benefits. Raising the minimum wage as an alternative to tax credits is a simple, effective and considerably fairer method of addressing the growing numbers of working poor families. However, there is also an urgent need to address the patterns of inequalities sustained through increasing 'flexploitation' (Gray 2004) of the labour market. Women and ethnic minorities are the most likely to depend on part-time, insecure, low-status, badly paid work. With the part-time gender pay gap in the UK still running at 41 per cent (Women and Equality Unit 2005), many working-class mothers are forced to choose between looking after their children full time on inadequate welfare benefits or arranging alternative care while they undertake hard labour for an unfair wage.

The limited and conditional financial assistance available to parents reveals the contradictory nature of family policy in the UK. Although parenting is heralded as a crucial 'job' requiring particular skills and training, full-time motherhood is not perceived to deserve any financial benefit. On the contrary, lone mothers who opt to stay at home must cope on subsistence-level benefits, while fulfilling an obligation to attend regular advice sessions on how to enter the labour market. Prevailing concerns about welfare state dependency reflect an assumption that parenting is a personal responsibility, while government policy-makers continue to assert the public significance of 'good' childrearing. An alternative approach involves recognising mothering as an intensive, demanding but extremely valuable social task.

As Selma James, founder of the Wages for Housework campaign in the 1970s, highlights, a large part of the work women do is unwaged and undervalued, providing no benefits, pension rights, health and safety protection or organised hours. She argues that full-time carers are entitled to financial recompense to enable them to choose how they organise their lives:

> What's so enriching about working in call centres? The only other choice: to scrimp on benefits or depend on a man, with no money of your own – a major source of domestic violence, including rape in marriage. I don't think most jobs men do are more important than raising children. Nor do I think women should be institutionalised as carers or men deprived of their kids. Time for a change! In Norway and Finland parents use the money from governments to pay others or do the caring themselves. This gives women bargaining power, to accept or reject what employers offer in wages and conditions. Power at home too: men either share the work or move on.
>
> (James and Benn 2004)

In the same article, Melissa Benn points to the risk of resurrecting old sociobiological claims that women are designed for caring and men for earning, thereby marginalising women from the world of employment. Nevertheless, there is a strong moral case to be made for substantially increasing welfare benefit payments to parents who want or need to draw them. Not only do full-time carers deserve recognition of their vital contribution to the capitalist economy, but the reduction of child poverty is dependent on making available greater financial resources to the poorest of families. As many commentators note, increased provision of direct economic support is the only way the UK government will be able to fulfil its pledge to eradicate child poverty (Fabian Commission on Life Chances and Child Poverty 2006; Middleton 2005; TUC 2003). Also, as Selma James points out, access to a regular and adequate income better enables women to protect themselves and their children from violence and abuse in the home. As I have shown, working-class mothers are particularly vulnerable in such situations and can suffer great hardship and stress in their struggle for safety and stability. Finding a decent and secure place to live is crucial precursor to re-building family lives, yet domestic violence remains a major cause of homelessness (Shelter 2004b).

To argue for increased welfare entitlement for parents is not to detract from the equally important need for widely available and affordable childcare. This practical form of support remains imperative for parents who want to work, re-train, or who may need particular help as a result of illness or special needs. While working-class mothers are often the targets for unwanted advice and education, their needs for more practical support and specialist services often go unmet. When specific problems are encountered with a child's health or education, mothers often find that help can be very difficult to obtain. In many parts of the country there are long waiting lists for appointments with speech therapists, educational psychologists, occupational therapists, child psychologists and other specialist services. In addition, seemingly mundane issues such as broken lifts in tower blocks, lack of play spaces and other facilities for children, isolation from shops and amenities, and other problems associated with deprived communities are rarely prioritised by governments, even though they impact heavily on everyday family life

Conclusion: identifying and legitimising working-class perspectives

This book has explored the experiences, practices and values of working-class mothers. In highlighting the complex, multifaceted and situated nature of their lives, it represents a serious challenge to the pathologising and disrespectful discourses which currently position them. Ruth Sidel describes statistics as 'people with the tears washed off' (Sidel 1992: xxiv). I hope this book demonstrates that the statistics representing marginalised mothers obscure far more than just tears. While the mothers struggled, worried and hurt, they also laughed, cherished and loved. In fact, it is difficult to convey the extent to which their warmth, humour, resilience and positive spirit dominated in the face of their often demanding and difficult lives. It is important to identify and counter disparaging assumptions and accusations, but it is also important not to mis-represent working-class mothers as passive victims.

As I have demonstrated, the mothers in this book actively constructed their family lives within the limited framework of choices and opportunities accessible to them. Their desires, actions and decisions were guided by internalised moral and practical dispositions or 'habitus' which ensured they survived and made the best of the resources they had access to. This analysis of real working-class lives highlights the extent to which professional discourses around parenting skills and child development are grounded in middle-class advantage. Also revealed is the way a culturally dominant mis-representation and denigration of working-class mothering practices works to justify the unjustifiable. The working classes are portrayed as ignorant, morally week and undeserving, thereby legitimating the entitlement of those who retain and pass on privilege through the generations. The morally troubling nature and consequences of inequality in prosperous Western nations cannot be addressed until this myth is successfully confronted.

I end this book by re-asserting the significance of class as a key theoretical concept. While such social categorisation risks overlaying and distorting the complexity of everyday life, it fulfils an essential pragmatic role as conceptual tool. It allows us to see the systemised way in which working-class mothers are denied access to resources others take for granted. Without recourse to class as an explanatory framework, the standpoints and experiences I have highlighted throughout the book might appear fragmented, shaped by local or personal concerns. This is not to downplay the diversity of working-class experience, investment and interests. Nor is it to overlook the way class is fused with other structural and institutionalised categories such as gender and race. For the mothers in this study, a common experience of economic and social marginalisation, vulnerability and powerlessness was lived out differently and specifically. The recognition that working-class women are oppressed in variety of ways highlights the importance of questioning essentialisms and assumptions. More significantly, this kind of class-based analysis provides an insight into how inequality is actually experienced and resisted, generating a more inclusive and realistic basis for empowerment and change.

References

Adkins, L. and Skeggs B. (2005) *Feminism after Bourdieu*. Oxford: Blackwell.

Allatt, P. (1993) 'Becoming privileged: the role of family processes', in I. Bates and G. Risebourough (eds), *Youth and Inequality*. Buckingham: Open University Press.

Alldred, P. (1996) 'Fit to parent? Developmental Psychology and "Non-traditional" Families', in E. Burman, P. Alldred, C. Bewley, B. Goldberg, C. Heenan, D. Marks, J. Marshall, K. Taylor, R. Ullah and S. Warner (eds), *Challenging Women: Psychology's Exclusions, Feminist Possibilities*. Buckingham: Open University Press.

Allegretto, S. A. (2005) 'Working families' incomes often fail to meet living expenses around the US', Briefing Paper #165, Washington, DC: Economic Policy Institute.

Allen, G. (2004) Letter to the *Guardian*, 26 November.

Anthias, F. (2005) 'Social stratification and social inequality: models of inter-sectionality and identity', in F. Devine, M. Savage, J. Scott and R. Crompton (eds), *Rethinking Class: Culture, Identities and Lifestyle*. Basingstoke: Paulgrave.

Argyle, M. (1994) *The Psychology of Social Class*. London: Routledge.

Aries, P. (1962) *Centuries of Childhood*. London: Cape.

Back, L. and Ware, V. (2001) *Out of Whiteness: Color, Politics and Culture*. Chicago, IL: University of Chicago Press.

Bagnell, G., Longhurst, B. and Savage, M. (2003) 'Children, belonging and social capital: the PTA and middle-class narratives of social involvement in the North-West of England', *Sociological Research Online*, 8 (4). Available online at http://www.socresonline.org.uk/8/4/bagnall.html

Ball, S.J. (2003) *Class Strategies and the Educational Market: The Middle Classes and Social Advantage*. London: RoutledgeFalmer.

BBC News Online (2001) 'Heads call for 'beacon' parents', Friday 1 June, http://news.bbc.co.uk/1/hi/education/1364234.stm accessed 7 August 2006.

BBC News Online (2005) 'Head teachers complain of abuse', Friday, 29 April, http://news.bbc.co.uk/1/hi/education/4493881.stm accessed 9/8/06.

Beck, U. (1992) *Risk Society: Towards a New Modernity*, London: Sage.

Beck, U. and Beck-Gernsheim, E. (1995) *The Normal Chaos of Love*, Cambridge: Polity Press.

Beck, U. and Beck-Gernsheim E. (2002) *Individualization*, London: Sage.

Benhabib, S. (1986) *Critique, Norm and Utopia*, New York: Columbia University Press.

Billig, M., Condor, S., Edwards, D., Gane, M., Middleton, D. and Radley, A. (1988) *Ideological Dilemmas*. London: Sage.

Blair, T. (2005) Speech at the Meridian Community Centre in Watford, 2 September, http://www.number10.gov.uk/output/Page8123.asp accessed 7/8/06.

Bonnett, A. (2000) *White Identities: Historical and International Perspectives*. Harlow: Prentice Hall.

Bordo, S. (1990) 'Feminism, postmodernism and gender scepticism', in L. Nicholson (ed), *Feminism and Postmodernism*. New York: Routledge.

Bordo, S. (1998) 'Bringing body to theory', in D. Welton (ed), *Body and Flesh: A Philosophical Reader*. Oxford: Blackwell.

Bourdieu, P. (1977) *Outline of a Theory of Practice*. Cambridge: Cambridge University Press.

Bourdieu, P. (1979) *Distinction: A Social Critique of the Judgement of Taste*. London: Routledge.

Bourdieu, P. (1990) *In Other Words: Essays Towards a Reflexive Sociology*. Cambridge: Polity Press.

Bourdieu, P. and Passeron, J. (1977) *Reproduction in Education, Society and Culture*. London: Sage.

Boyden, J. (1990) 'Childhood and the policy makers: a comparative perspective on the globalization of childhood', in A. James and A. Prout (eds), *Constructing and Reconstructing Childhood: Contemporary Issues in the Sociological Study of Childhood*. Basingstoke: Falmer.

Bruegel, I. and Gray, A. (2004) 'The future of work and the division of childcare between parents', *Social Science Research Paper 18*. London: London South Bank University.

Bullen, E., Kenway, J. and Hey, V. (2000) 'New Labour, social exclusion and educational risk management: the case of "gymslip mums"', *British Educational Research Journal*, 26 (4), 441–56.

Bunting, M. (2004) 'The myth of Billy Elliot', *Guardian*, Monday 22 November.

Burman, E. (1994) *Deconstructing Developmental Psychology*. London: Routledge.

Burman, E. (1996) 'Introduction: Contexts contests and interventions', in E. Burman, P. Alldred, C. Bewley, B. Goldberg, C. Heenan, D. Marks, J. Marshall, K. Taylor, R. Ullah and S. Warner (eds), *Challenging Women: Psychology's Exclusions, Feminist Possibilities*. Buckingham: Open University Press.

Byrne, B. (2006) *White Lives: The Interplay of 'Race', Class and Gender in Everyday Life*. London: Routledge.

Charlesworth, S. (2000) *A Phenomenology of Working Class Experience*. Cambridge: Cambridge University Press.

Children and Adoption Bill (2005) www.publications.parliament.uk/pa/ld200506/ldbills/010/2006010.htm accessed 23/5/06.

Civitas (2002) *Experiments in Living: The Fatherless Family*. London: Civitas.

Clarke, N. (2001) 'Single Mother Central', *Daily Mail*, 12 May.

Clarke, L. (2005) 'Heads want power to expel children of violent parents', *Daily Mail*, 6 July, http://www.dailymail.co.uk/pages/live/articles/news/news.html?in_article_id=354792&in_page_id=1770 accessed 9/8/06.

Cole, M. (2004) '"Brutal and stinking" and "difficult to handle": the historical and contemporary manifestations of racialisation, institutional racism, and schooling in Britain', *Race, Ethnicity and Education*, 7 (1), 35–56.

Collishaw, S., Maughan, B., Goodman, R. and Pickles, A. (2004) 'Time trends in adolescent mental health', *Journal of Child Psychology and Psychiatry*, 45 (8), 1350–63.

Cook, D. (1997) *Poverty, Crime and Punishment*. London: Child Poverty Action Group.

Crime and Disorder Act (1998), London: HMSO. http://www.opsi.gov.uk/acts/acts 1998/19980037.htm accessed 9/8/06.

Daly, M. and Wilson, M. (1999) *The Truth About Cinderella: A Darwinian View of Parental Love*. London: Weidenfeld and Nicolson.

Davis, A. (1981) *Women, Race and Class*. London: The Women's Press.

Davies, J. (1993) *The Family, is it Just Another Lifestyle Choice?* London: Institute For Economic Affairs.

Dench, G., Gavron, K. and Young, M. (2006) *The New East End: Kinship, Race and Conflict*. London: Profile.

Dennis, N. and Erdos, G. (1992) *Families Without Fatherhood*. London: Institute for Economic Affairs.

Department for Education and Skills (2005) *Ethnicity and Education: The Evidence on Minority Ethnic Pupils*, London: DfES Research Topic Paper. http://www.dfes. gov.uk/research/data/uploadfiles/RTP01-05.pdf accessed 23/1/06.

Department for Work and Pensions (2005), *Households Below Average Income 1994/95 to 2003/04*. Corporate Document Services, Table 3.5.

Devine, F. and Savage, M. (2005) 'The cultural turn, sociology and class analysis', in F. Devine, M. Savage, J. Scott and R. Crompton (eds), *Rethinking Class: Culture, Identities and Lifestyle*. Basingstoke: Palgrave.

Donzelot, J. (1979) *The Policing of Families*. London: Hutchinson.

Drakeford, M. (1996) 'Parents of young people in trouble', *Howard Journal*, 35 (3), 242–55.

Duncan, S. (1995) 'Mothering, class and rationality', *Sociological Review*, 53 (2), 49–76.

Duncan, S. and Edwards, R. (1999) *Lone Mothers, Paid Work and Gendered Rationalities*. London: Macmillan.

Duncan, S. and Edwards, R. (2003) 'State welfare regimes, mothers' agencies and gendered moral rationalities', in K. Kollind and A. Peterson (eds), *Thoughts on Family, Gender, Generation and Class: A Festschrift to Ulla Björnberg*. Göteborg: Sociologiska Institutionen, Göteborgs Universitet.

Dwyer, P. (2002) 'Making sense of social citizenship: some user views on welfare rights and responsibilities', *Critical Social Policy*, 22 (2), 273–99.

EducationGuardian (2003) 'Exams taking their toll on children', 25 April. www.education.guardian.co.uk/schools/story/0,5500,943430,00.html accessed 7/6/06.

Edwards, R. (1996) 'White woman researcher – black women subjects', in S. Wilkinson and C. Kitzinger (eds), *Representing the Other*. London: Sage.

Edwards, R. and Alldred, P. (2000) 'A typology of parental involvement in education centring on children and young people: negotiating familialisation, institution-alisation and individualisation', *British Journal of Sociology of Education*, 21 (4), 435–55.

Edwards, R. and Gillies V. (2004) 'Support in parenting: values and consensus concerning who to turn to', *Journal of Social Policy*, 33 (4), 623–43.

Edwards, R. and Gillies, V. (2005) 'Resources in Parenting: Access to Capitals Project Report', Families & Social Capital ESRC Research Report No14. London: South Bank University.

Edwards, R., Franklin, J. and Holland, J. (2003) 'Families and Social Capital: Exploring the Issues', Families & Social Capital ESRC Research Group Working Paper No. 1. London: South Bank University.

Ehrenreich, B. (2001) *Nickel and Dimed: On (Not) Getting By in America*. New York: Metropolitan Books.

Etzoni, A. (1994) *The Spirit of Community*. New York: Crown.

Everingham, C. (2003) *Justice and the Politics of Community*. Aldershot: Ashgate.

Fabian Commission on Life Chances and Child Poverty (2006) *Narrowing the Gap: A Manifesto to Make Britain More Equal*. London: Fabian Society.

Fairclough, N. (2000) *New Labour, New Language*. London: Routledge.

Farrington, D. (1996) *Understanding and Preventing Youth Crime*. York: York Publishing Services.

Featherstone, B. and Trinder, L. (2001) 'New Labour, Families and Fathers', *Critical Social Policy*, 21 (4), 534–6.

Fevre, R. (2000) *The Demoralisation of Western Culture*. London: Continuum.

Field, F. (2004) 'Interview with Paul Dornan', *Poverty*, (Winter), 117.

Finch, L (1993) *The Classing Gaze: Sexuality, Class and Surveillance*. St Leonards, Australia: Allen and Unwin.

Finch, J. (1994) 'Do families support each other more or less than in the past?', in M. Drake (ed.), *Time, Family and Community*. Oxford: Blackwell.

Fine, M. and Weis, L. (1998) *The Unknown City: The Lives of Poor and Working-class Young Adults*. Boston, MA: Beacon.

Firth, R. (1956) *Two Studies of Kinship in London*. London: Athlone.

Firth, R., Hubert, J. and Forge, A. (1969) *Families and Their Relatives*. London: Routledge and Kegan Paul.

Flaherty, J., Viet-Willson, J. and Dorman, P. (2004) *Poverty, the Facts*, 5th edn. London: Child Poverty Action Group.

Foucault, M (1979) *Discipline and Punish*. Harmondsworth: Penguin.

Fox Harding, L. (2000) 'Supporting families/controlling families – towards a characterisation of New Labour's family policy', Working Paper 21. Leeds: Centre for Research on Family Kinship and Childhood.

Frankenberg, R. (1993) *White Women, Race Matters: The Social Construction of Whiteness*. Minneapolis, MN: Routledge.

Fraser, N. (1997) *Justice Interruptus: Critical Reflections on the "Postsocialist" Condition*. London: Routledge.

Furedi, F. (2001) *Paranoid Parenting*. London: Penguin.

Furlong, A. and Cartmel, F. (1997) *Young People and Social Change: Individualisation and Risk in Late Modernit*. Buckingham: Open University Press.

Garner, S. (2006) 'The uses of whiteness: what sociologists working in Europe can draw from US research on whiteness,' *Sociology*, 40 (2), 257–75.

Gewirtz, S. (2001) 'Cloning the Blairs: New Labour's programme for the re-socialization of working-class parents', *Journal of Education Policy*,16 (4), 365–78.

Giddens, A. (1991) *Modernity and Self-identity: Self and Society in the Late Modern Age*. Cambridge: Polity Press.

Giddens, A. (1992) *The Transformation of Intimacy: Sexuality, Love and Eroticism in Modern Societies*. Cambridge: Polity Press.

Giddens, A. (1998) *The Third Way: The Renewal of Social Democracy*. Cambridge: Polity Press.

Gillies, V. (2000) 'Young people and family life: analysing and comparing disciplinary discourses', *Journal of Youth Studies*, 3 (2), 211–28.

Gillies, V. (2004) 'Researching through working class personal networks: issues and dilemmas in bridging different worlds', in *Social Capital in the Field: Researchers Tales*. Families & Social Capital ESRC Research Group Working Paper No.10.

Gillies, V. (2005a) 'Meeting parents needs? Discourses of 'support' and 'inclusion' in family policy', *Critical Social Policy*, 25 (1), 70–91.

Gillies, V. (2005b) 'Raising the meritocracy: parenting and the individualisation of social class', *Sociology*, 39 (5), 835–52.

Gillies, V. (2006a) 'Working-class mothers and school life: exploring the role of emotional capital', *Gender and Education*, 18 (3), 281–93.

Gillies, V. (2006b) 'Parenting and social class: exploring the context of childrearing', *Community Practitioner*, 79 (4), 114–117.

Gillies, V. (2006c) 'Fathering in families: exploring parenting, gender and ideology from a UK perspective', ESRC research seminar: Fathers and Social Capital: Transatlantic Perspectives on Fathering, Support and Community Networks. Friday 26 May, London South Bank University.

Gillies, V. and Edwards, R. (2006) 'A qualitative analysis of parenting and social capital: comparing the work of Coleman and Bourdieu'. Under revision for forthcoming publication in *Qualitative Sociology*.

Gilligan, C. (1982) *In a Different Voice*. Cambridge, MA: Harvard University Press.

Goodhart, D. (2004) 'Too diverse', *Prospect* (February), 30–37.

Gorz, A. (1982) *Farewell to the Working Class: An Essay of Post Industrial Socialism*. London: Pluto

Graham, J. and Bowling, B. (1995) 'Understanding and preventing youth crime', Home Office Research Study 145. London: Home Office.

Gray, A. (2004) *Unsocial Europe: social protection or 'flexploitation'*. London: Pluto.

Griffin, C. (1996) ' "See whose face it wears": difference, otherness and power', in S. Wilkinson and C. Kitzinger (eds), *Representing the Other*. London: Sage.

Haylett, C. (2001) 'Illegitimate subjects? Abject whites, neoliberal modernism and middle-class multiculturalism', *Environment and Planning D: Society and Space*, 19 (3), 351–70.

Heffer, S. (2005) 'Shouldn't we jail the baby factory mum?', *Daily Mail*, 28 May.

Hendrick, H. (1990) 'Constructions and reconstructions of British childhood: an interpretive survey, 1800 to the present', in A. James and A. Prout (eds), *Constructing and Reconstructing Childhood: Contemporary Issues in the Sociological Study of Childhood*. Basingstoke: Falmer.

Henricson, C. (2003) 'Government and parenting: is there a case for a policy review and a parents code? York: York Publishing Services.

Hey, V. (2000) 'Troubling the auto/biography of the questions: re/thinking rapport and the politics of social class in feminist participant observation, genders and sexualities', *Educational Ethnography*, 3, 16–183.

Hill Collins, P. (1987) 'The meaning of motherhood in black culture and black mother–daughter relationships, *A Scholarly Journal on Black Women*, 4 (2), 3–10.

Hill Collins, P. (1990) *Black Feminist Thought: Knowledge, Consciousness and the Politics of Empowerment*. Boston, MA: Unwin Hyman.

Hill Collins, P. (1994) 'Shifting the centre: race, class and feminist theorising about motherhood', in E. Glen, G. Chang and L. Forcey (eds), *Mothering: Ideology, Experiences and Agency*. Boston, MA: Unwin Hyman.

Hodge, M. (2004a) Speech to the Social Market Foundation, Social Market Foundation, London, 1 May.

Hodge, M. (2004b) Speech to the Institute for Public Policy Research (IPPR), London, 26 November.

Home Office (1998) *Boys, Young Men and Fathers: A Ministerial Seminar*. London: HMSO.

Home Office (2003a) *Every Child Matters*. London: HMSO.

Home Office (2003b) *Respect and Responsibility: Taking a Stand Against Anti-Social Behaviour*. London: HMSO.

hooks, b. (1989) *Talking Back: Thinking Feminist – Thinking Black*. London: Sheba Feminist Publishers.

hooks, b. (1999) *Aint I a Woman*. Boston, MA: South End Press.

hooks, b. (2000) *Where We Stand: Class Matters*. New York: Routledge.

Institute for Fiscal Studies (2006) *Poverty and Inequality in Britain*. London: IFS.

James, A., Jenks, C. and Prout, A. (1998) *Theorizing Childhood*. Cambridge: Polity Press.

James, S. and Benn, M. (2004) 'Home truths for feminists', *Guardian*, Saturday 21 February, http://www.guardian.co.uk/comment/story/0,,1152715,00.html accessed 9/8/06.

Jenkins, R. (1992) *Pierre Bourdieu*. London: Routledge

Jenks, Chris (1996) *Childhood*. London: Routledge.

Joseph, K. (1975) 'The cycle of deprivation', in E. Butterworth and R. Holman (eds), *Social Welfare in Modern Britain*. Glasgow: Fontana.

Kirk, J. (2006) 'Marking the moral boundaries of class', *Sociological Research Online*, 11 (1), http://www.socresonline.org.uk/11/1/kirk.html accessed 31/5/06.

Kirkman, M., Harrison, L., Hillier, L. and Pyett, P. (2001) 'I know I'm doing a good job': canonical and autobiographical narratives of teenage mothers. *Culture, Health & Sexuality*, 3 (3), 279–94.

Kitzinger, C. and Wilkinson, S. (1996) 'Theorizing representing the other', in S. Wilkinson and C. Kitzinger (eds), *Representing the Other*. London: Sage.

Lareau, A. (2003) *Unequal Childhoods, Class, Race and Family Life*. Berkeley, CA: University of California Press.

Lasch, C. (1977) *Haven in a Heartless World*. New York: Basic Books.

Law, A. (2006) 'Hatred and respect: the class shame of Ned "Humour"', *Variant*, issue 25, http://www.variant.randomstate.org/25texts/nedhumour25.html accessed 31/5/06.

Lawler, S. (2000) *Mothering the Self: Mothers, Daughters, Subjects*. London: Routledge.

Lawler, S. (2005) 'Disgusted subjects: the making of middle-class identities', *Sociological Review*, 53 (3), 429–46.

Levitas, R. (1998) *The Inclusive Society: Social Exclusion and New Labour*. Basingstoke: Macmillan.

Lucey, H. and Reay, D. (2002) 'Carrying the beacon of excellence: social class differentiation and anxiety at a time of transition', *Journal of Education Policy*, 17 (3), 321–36.

McDonald, R., Shildrick, T., Webster, C. and Simpson, D. (2005) 'Growing up in poor neighbourhoods: the significance of class and place in the extended transitions of socially excluded young adults', *Sociology*, 39 (5), 873–93.

McRobbie, A. (2001) 'Good girls, bad girls? Female success and the new meritocracy', in D. Morley and K. Robins (eds), *British Cultural Studies*, Oxford: Oxford University Press.

McRobbie, A. (2006) 'Yummy mummies leave a bad taste for young women', *Guardian*, Thursday 2 March.

Mead, L. (1986) *Beyond Entitlement: The Social Obligations of Citizenship*. New York: Free Press.

Middleton, S. (2005) 'The adequacy of benefits for children', in G. Preston (ed.), *At Greatest Risk: The Children Most Likely to be Poor*. London: Child Poverty Action Group.

Mirza, H. (1995) 'Black women in higher education: defining a space/finding a place', in Mirza, H. (ed), *Feminist Academics: Creative Agents for Change*. London: Taylor and Francis.

Mitchell, W. and Green, E. (2002) '"I don't know what I'd do without our Mam": motherhood, identity and support networks', *The Sociological Review*, 50 (1), 1–22 .

Moran, P., Ghate, D. and van der Merwe, A. (2004) *What Works in Parenting Support? A Review of the International Evidence*. London: Policy Research Bureau.

Morris, E. (2002) Speech to the Association of Teachers and Lecturers' annual conference, Cardiff, 28 March.

Morris, L. (1994) *Dangerous Classes: The Underclass and Social Citizenship*. London: Routledge.

Murray, C. (1994) *Underclass: The Crisis Deepens*. London: Institute of Economic Affairs.

New Policy Institute (2006) 'Monitoring poverty and social exclusion', http://www.poverty.org.uk/intro/index.htm accessed 1/6/06.

Notwotny, H. (1981) 'Women in public life in Austria', in C. Fuchs Epstein and R. Laub Coser (eds), *Access to Power: Cross-National Studies of Women and Elites*. London: Sage.

Osborne, A. F. and Morris, T.C. (1979) 'The rationale for a composite index of social class and its evaluation', *British Journal of Sociology*, 30, 39–60.

Palmer, G., Carr, J. and Kenway, P. (2005) *Monitoring Poverty and Social Exclusion*, York: Joseph Rowntree Foundation.

Parker, I. (1992) *Discourse Dynamics Critical Analysis for Social and Individual Psychology*. London: Routledge.

Phoenix, A. and Wollett, A. (1991) 'Motherhood: social construction, politics and psychology', in A. Phoenix, A. Woollett and E. Lloyd (eds), *Motherhood: Meanings, Practices and Ideologies*. London: Sage.

Prior, D. and Paris, A. (2005) 'Preventing children's involvement in crime and anti-social behaviour: a literature review', DfES Research Report RR623. Birmingham: DfES.

Proweller, A. (2000) 'Re-writing/-righting lives: voices of pregnant and parenting teenagers in an alternative school', in L. Weis and M. Fine (eds), *Construction*

Sites: Excavating Race, Class, and Gender Among Urban Youth, New York: Teachers College Press, pp. 100–120.

Ramazanoglu, C. and Holland, J. (1999) 'Tripping over experience: some problems in feminist epistemology', *Discourse: Studies in the Cultural Politics of Education*, 20 (3), 381–92.

Reay, D. (1995) '"They employ cleaners to do that": habitus in the primary classroom', *British Journal of Sociology of Education*, 16 (3), 353–71.

Reay, D. (1996) 'Dealing with difficult differences: reflexivity and social class in feminist research', *Feminism and Psychology*, 6 (3), 443–56.

Reay, D. (1997) 'Feminist theory, habitus and social class: disrupting notions of classlessness', *Women's Studies International Forum*, 20 (2), 225–33.

Reay, D. (1998) *Class Work: Mother's Involvement in Their Children's Primary Schooling*. London: UCL Press.

Reay, D. (2000) 'A useful extension of Bourdieu's conceptual framework? Emotional capital as a way of understanding mother's involvement in their children's education?', *Sociological Review*, 48 (4), 568–85.

Reay, D. (2002) 'Gendering Bourdieu's concept of capitals?: emotional capital, women and social class', Paper given at Feminists Evaluate Bourdieu: International Perspectives Conference, Manchester, 11 October, http://www.bris.ac.uk/educa tion/research/esrc_seminar/papers/2_1ReayEmotlabour.pdf accessed 22/8/05.

Reay, D. (2005a) 'Beyond consciousness? The psychic landscape of social class', *Sociology*, 39 (5), 911–29.

Reay, D. (2005b) 'Doing the dirty work of social class? Mothers' work in support of their children's schooling', in M. Glucksmann, L. Pettinger and J. West (eds), *A New Sociology of Work*. Oxford: Blackwell.

Reay, D. and Lucey, H. (2000) 'Children, school choice and social differences', *Educational Studies*, 26 (1), 83–100.

Reynolds, T. (1997) 'Class matters, "race" matters, gender matters', in P. Mahony and C. Zmroczek (eds), *Class Matters: Working-Class Women's Perspectives on Social Class*. London: Taylor and Francis.

Reynolds, T. (2005) *Caribbean Mothers. Identity and Experience in the UK*. London: Tufnell.

Ribbens, J. (1994) *Mothers and Their Children: A Feminist Sociology of Childrearing*. London: Sage.

Ribbens McCarthy, J. and Edwards, R. (2002) 'The individual in public and private: the significance of mothers and children', in A. Carling, S. Duncan and R. Edwards (eds), *Analysing Families: Morality and Rationality in Policy and Practice*. London: Routledge.

Ribbens McCarthy, J., Edwards, R. and Gillies, V. (2003) *Making Families: Moral Tales of Parenting and Step-parenting*. Durham: Sociology Press.

Robbins, D. (2001) 'Transforming children's services: an evaluation of local responses to the Quality Protects Programme, Year 3: London: Department of Health.

Rodger, J. (1995) 'Family policy or moral regulation?', *Critical Social Policy*, 15, 5–25.

Rose, N. (1999) *Governing the Soul: The Shaping of the Private Self*. London: Routledge.

Rose, N. (2002) *Powers of Freedom: Reframing Political Thought*. Cambridge: Cambridge University Press.

Rosser, C. and Harris, C. (1965) *The Family and Social Change*. London: Routledge and Kegan Paul.

Rowlands, M. (2005) 'The state of ASBO Britain – the rise of intolerance', Essays for Civil Liberties and Democracy in Europe, European Civil Liberties Network www.asboconcern.org.uk

Savage, M. (2000) *Class Analysis and Social Transformation*. Buckingham: Open University Press.

Sayer, A. (2005) *The Moral Significance of Class*. Cambridge: Cambridge University Press.

Scourfield, J. and Drakeford, M. (2002) 'New Labour and the "Problem of Men"', *Critical Social Policy*, 22 (4), 619–40.

Sennett, R. (1998) *The Corrosion of Character: The Personal Consequences of Work in New Capitalism*. New York: Norton.

Sevenhuijsen, S. (2002) 'A third way? Moralities, ethics and families: an approach through the ethic of care', in A. Carling, S. Duncan and R. Edwards (eds), *Analysing Families: Morality and Rationality in Policy and Practice*. London: Routledge.

Seymour, S. (1999) *Women, Family and Child Care in India: A World in Transition*. Cambridge: Cambridge University Press.

Shelter (2004a) 'Consultation response: safety and justice', www.shelter.org.uk accessed 7/6/06.

Shelter (2004b) *Toying with Their Future: The Hidden Cost of the Housing Crisis*. London: Shelter.

Shirk, M., Bennett N. G. and Aber, J. M. (1999) *Lives on the Line: American Families and the Struggle to Make Ends Meet*. Boulder, CO : Westview.

Shulman, B. (2003) *The Betrayal of Work : How Low-Wage Jobs Fail 30 Million Americans and Their Families*. New York: New Press.

Sidel, R. (1992) *Women and Children Last: The Plight of Poor Women in Affluent America*. New York: Penguin.

Skeggs, B. (1997) *Formations of Class and Gender*. London: Sage.

Skeggs, B. (2004) *Class, Self, Culture*. London: Routledge.

Skeggs, B. (2005) 'The making of class and gender through visualizing moral subject formation', *Sociology*, 39 (5), 965–82.

Stanley, L. and Wise, S. (1993) *Breaking Out Again*. London: Routledge.

Townsend, P. (1957) *Family Life of Older People: An Inquiry in East London*. London: Penguin.

Toynbee, P. (2003) *Hard Work: Life in Low-pay Britain*. London: Bloomsbury.

Toynbee, P. (2004) 'Our subsidy to low pay', *Guardian*, Friday 29 October.

Treasury (2000) 'Brown launches pre-budget report consultation tour, setting new targets to help lone parents get into work', Press Release, 9 October 2000.

TUC (2003) 'Benefits and tax credits must increase to end child poverty', http://www.tuc.org.uk/welfare/tuc-7386-f0.cfm accessed 7/6/06.

Turney, J. (1999) 'Human nature totally explained', *Times Higher*, 12 March.

Utting, W. (1997) 'People like us: the report of the Review of Safeguards for Children Living Away from Home,' London: Department of Health/Welsh Office, The Stationery Office.

van Dijk, T. A. (1993) *Elite Discourse and Racism*. Newbury Park, CA: Sage.

Vincent, C. (2000) *Including Parents? Education, Citizenship and Parental Agency*. Buckingham: Open University Press.

Walkerdine, V. (1996) 'Working-class women: psychological and social aspects of survival', in S. Wilkinson (ed.), *Feminist Social Psychologies: International Perspectives*. Buckingham: Open University Press, pp. 145–62.

Walkerdine, V. and Lucey, H. (1989) *Democracy in the Kitchen*, London: Virago Press.

Walkerdine, V., Lucey, H. and Melody, J. (2001) *Growing Up Girl: Psychosocial Explorations of Gender and Class*. Basingstoke: Palgrave.

Ward, J. and Pearson, G. (2003) 'Tracking care leavers as they move to independence', ESRC Research Report, http://www.regard.ac.uk/research_findings/R000223982/report.pdf accessed 15/10/05.

Ward, J., Henderson, Z., Pearson, G. (2003) 'One problem among many: drug use among care leavers in transition to independent living', *Home Office Research Study 260*. London: Home Office.

Wasoff, F. and Hill, M. (2002) 'Family policy in Scotland', *Social Policy and Society*, 1 (3), 171–82.

Wetherell, M. and Potter, J. (1992) *Mapping the Language of Racism: Discourse and the Legitimisation of Exploitation*. Englewood Cliffs, NJ: Prentice Hall.

Wheeler, B., Shaw, M., Mitchel, R. and Dorling, D. (2005) *Life in Britain: Using Millennial Census Data to Understand Poverty, Inequality and Place*. Bristol: The Policy Press.

Willis, P. (1977) *Learning to Labour: How Working-Class Kids get Working-Class Jobs*. London: Hutchinson.

Williams, F. (1998) 'Troubmasculinities in social policy discourses: fatherhood', in J. Popay, J. Hearn and J. Edwards (eds), *Men, Gender Divisions and Welfare*. London: Routledge.

Women and Equality Unit (2005) 'What is the Pay Gap and why does it exist?', http://www.womenandequalityunit.gov.uk/pay/pay_facts.htm accessed 8/8/06.

Woodhead, M. (1997) 'Psychology and the cultural construction of children's needs', in A. James and A. Prout (eds), *Constructing and Reconstructing Childhood*. London: Falmer.

Youdell, D. (2003) 'Identity traps or how black students fail: the interactions between biographical, sub-cultural, and learner identities', *British Journal of Sociology of Education*, 24 (1), 3–20.

Youdell, D. (2004) 'Engineering school markets, constituting schools and subjectivating students: the bureaucratic, institutional and classroom dimensions of educational triage', *Journal of Education Policy*,19 (4), 407–432.

Young, J. (1999) *The Exclusive Society, Crime and Difference in Late Modernity*. London: Sage.

Young, M. and Willmott, P. (1957) *Family and Kinship in East London*. London: Routledge and Kegan Paul.

Younge, G. (2005) 'Left to sink or swim', *Guardian*, Monday 5 September.

Youth Justice Board, http://www.youth-justice-board.gov.uk/PractitionersPortal/PracticeAndPerformance/Performance/AnnualStatistics/ accessed 9/8/06.

Index

vulnerability 68–9, 121, 146; and power 100, 102, 103–9

Walkerdine, V. *et al.* 10, 25, 33–4, 76, 83, 151, 153–4, 155, 157
welfare benefits 5, 43, 45, 46, 47–56, 59, 60, 62–3, 157, 158
welfare policy: opportunities *vs.* aid 23; reform 42–3; workfare 43
Wetherell, M. 25
whiteness 30–1
Wilkinson, S. 15
Willis, P. 38
Wilson, M. 56
'Women Empowering Women' 67
women's liberation 5
workfare 43
working class 22; coded representations 25–6; racism 31; solidarity 71–3, 75, 92, 95; stereotypes 26–7, 33; subjectivity 70, 75; whiteness 30–1; women 26–7
working-class mothers: becoming a mum 118–19; being a single mother 119–21, 125–6, 142; emotional capital 17–18, 97, 127, 128–32, 135, 142, 144–5, 159; gender and commitment 135–42; identity 18; mediating trauma and impoverishment 122–7; and pregnant young daughters 27–8; stereotypes 27–8, 142; values 44, 77, 146

Youdell, D. 110, 112
Young, J. 24
Younge, G. 29
Youth Justice Board 147

More titles in the Relationships and Resources Series

Sibling Identity and Relationships
Sisters and Brothers

Rosalind Edwards, Lucy Hadfield, Helen Lucey
and Melanie Mauthner

What does it mean to be a sister or a brother, and are such relationships born or made? What do children and young people see as the defining features of their sibling relationships, and how does this relate to social context?

Sibling Identity and Relationships explores the special place that siblings occupy in the lives of children and young people and provides new insights into sibling identity and relationships. Drawing on social constructionist and psychodynamic perspectives, it discusses who constitutes a sibling, emotional connections and separations, conflict and aggression and how siblings construct and conduct their relationship out of the home, at school and in local communities.

Sibling Identity and Relationships explores the ways that siblings are important for children and young people's social and emotional sense of self in relation to others, throwing light on broader debates about social and psychic divisions in wider society. This book will appeal to academics and students of childhood studies and social work as well as health and social care professionals.

Hbk 978–0–415–33929–2
Pbk 978–0–415–33930–8

Teenagers and Citizenship
Experiences and Education

Susie Weller

Can citizenship education stem declining civic engagement and social capital or do we need to view these concepts in new ways? Can citizenship education overcome teenage apathy or are teenagers engaged in new or alternative forms of participation?

The introduction of compulsory citizenship education into the national curriculum has generated a plethora of new interests in the politics of childhood and youth. This book explores teenagers' acts of and engagement with citizenship in their local communities and examines the role of citizenship education in creating future responsible citizens.

Susie Weller's important book will throw new light on how teenagers engage with citizenship education and take on civic responsibility. It is an interesting and useful read for all those involved with education and youth policy as well as those studying for a PGCE or researching in citizenship education.

Hbk 978–0–415–40463–1
Pbk 978–0–415–40464–8

Moving On
The Changing Lives of Young People
after Parental Divorce

Bren Neale and Jennifer Flowerdew

This book is based on a qualitative, longitudinal study of the lives of a group of young people with divorced parents, and the multiple resources (social, emotional and material) that they use in managing changes and continuities in their lives. Drawing on detailed family case histories spanning an eight year period, it explores 'who' and 'what' matters to young people of varied ages and backgrounds as they navigate changes within and beyond their families. In exploring these themes, the book sheds light on the dynamics of risk and resiliency and offers a radical reassessment of the place occupied by parental divorce in the lives of young people.

Hbk 978–0–415–36789–9
Pbk 978–0–415–36790–5

Available at all good bookshops
For ordering and further information please visit:
www.routledge.com